An Expert's Guide to

YOUR
RIGHT
FIRST JOB

T. Muralidharan, is a first generation entrepreneur, who established the TMI Group, which is among the top recruiting firms in India. A graduate of IIT Chennai and IIM Ahmedabad, Muralidharan started his company with an initial investment of ₹50,000 in 1987, and now has turnover of over ₹500 million. Over the years, he has helped over a hundred thousand professionals get jobs in the private corporate sector. He writes on issues related to career and employment in leading newspapers and magazines, including *The Hindu*, *The Week* and *Sakshi*. He is also the founder of JobsDialog, India's first exclusive recruitment platform for small and medium enterprises.

Reach him at: www.employabilityfirst.com

An Expert's Guide to

YOUR RIGHT FIRST JOB

T. Muralidharan

RUPA

Published by
Rupa Publications India Pvt. Ltd 2015
7/16, Ansari Road, Daryaganj
New Delhi 110002

Sales Centres:

Allahabad Bengaluru Chennai
Hyderabad Jaipur Kathmandu
Kolkata Mumbai

Copyright © T. Muralidharan 2015

ISBN: 978-81-291-3571-1

Third impression 2015

10 9 8 7 6 5 4 3

The moral right of the author has been asserted.

Printed by Thomson Press India Ltd, Faridabad

This book is dedicated to two people:
my wife Lalita Iyer and
my father, the late Shri G.T. Rajan

CONTENTS

INTRODUCTION

'There are many ways to skin a cat.' Well, this old saying applies to career success too. If you study the résumés of the most successful chief executive officers (CEOs) and members of leadership teams—and I have examined thousands of them as an executive recruiter—each of them adopted a different route to the top. However, the common factor among most of them was that they started their career with the Right First Job (RFJ).

What are the characteristics of an RFJ? How are you to find this magic job which can propel you to the top? Does the RFJ vary from person to person? If so, why does it vary? How does it vary?

When I talk to fresh graduates—and I must have met thousands—they want 'prescriptive' answers. My problem is that there is no simple and single answer to all these questions. Yes, there are some common inferences that we can draw from the success and failure stories of professionals; my experience in executive search has been of great help as well in the writing of this book.

In two peak years, TMI First—our division for fresher hiring—hired over 15,000 graduates and MBAs after visiting over 600 engineering, graduate and MBA campuses, and assessed over two lakh freshers. This knowledge of who these freshers were, and what they wanted, is the backbone of this book.

One of the learnings from this experience is that parents play a big role in helping their children in choosing the career. So the attempt here is to write for different target groups:

◻ students who are in their final year of graduation;
◻ young people who have just passed out of college and are looking for jobs;
◻ anyone with four years of experience, or less, who wants to change their existing job; and
◻ parents of the above.

Young people are very different from their parents in terms of both outlook and knowledge level. Parents like to know the theory and options, while youngsters want more decisive and prescriptwations. I have attempted to reach out to both these segments.

More than 2.5 million students graduate from college each year in India. There are those who are fortunate enough to get a job through campus recruitment, but others have to look for jobs after graduation. This is when the struggle begins. Many of them do not know which company to join, which industry to look for, what are the advantages of working overseas, etc.

This book also caters specifically to the needs of students stepping into the corporate world for the first time. It highlights the importance of knowing your personality, finding the right industry, how to choose the right first employer, and many such important aspects.

This book is designed to take graduates through all that they should know and do in order to land a job that is right for them; in other words, a job that matches their qualifications, personality, and preferences. It will also enable them to take advantage of the various job opportunities available in the market to build a good career.

It covers a wide range of topics and provides practical tips;

and goes beyond merely getting the RFJ. For instance, one chapter deals solely with the first ninety days on the first job, and discusses the management of this critical period. Overall, therefore, the thrust is on getting the RFJ and retaining it.

1

THE RIGHT FIRST JOB

Getting the Right First Job (RFJ) is crucial to your ensuing career success. So let's get on with understanding all the factors that go into making up your RFJ. Before we do that, let's understand what is a job and what do we mean by a job description.

Understanding a 'job' and 'job description'

What is a 'job'?

A job refers to an activity or a set of activities that an individual has to do in order to earn a salary. The focus in this book is on 'wage employment', where you are working for someone. There are thousands of jobs available in the market and you need to find a job depending on your qualifications, skills-set and experience.

What is a 'job description'?

A job description tells you your tasks (what you are expected to do), and your responsibilities (what you are expected to deliver).

Let us assume that there is a vacancy in a company for an accountant. The employer places a posting on the job boards but fails to explain what exactly the job entails. In a hurry to fill the position, the employer hires a BSc graduate just out of college. What happens? They ends up hiring a candidate who is not capable of doing the job, and the candidate ends up choosing the wrong first job. And he is fired.

Therefore, to avoid such issues, companies make it a point to explain the job description along with other details related to the job. The other details include listing the designation, the salary, the qualifications required to apply for the job, other skills they are looking for, and many other such details when posting a job vacancy on job boards. All these details are put together in what is known as a 'recruitment advertisement' or a 'job posting'.

A job description thus refers to a detailed description of the roles and responsibilities associated with a job, and every job has a job description.

It is extremely important for an individual to study the job description before applying for a job. It gives a complete picture of what the job is all about.

Let's illustrate this with an example of the job description of an accounts assistant that we referred to earlier:

JD of accounts assistant:

Accounts assistants provide support to accountants and are responsible for preparing accounting documents and entering the accounting transactions into computer software.

The duties and responsibilities of the job include:

- Working with accounting software, spreadsheets, sales and purchase ledgers and accounting journals;
- Preparing financial documents such as invoices, cheques, purchase orders, cash vouchers, etc.;
- Calculating and checking to make sure payments, amounts and records are correct;
- Maintaining statutory accounts;
- Reconciling accounts;
- Generating reports;

◻ Managing petty cash transactions;
◻ Controlling credit and chasing outstanding dues.

Now you can understand why a BSc graduate with no accounting experience will struggle and why a BCom graduate will enjoy this job.

How will a job description help you?

Every fresh graduate thinks that he/she can do any job; but you, the job-seeker, have to ask yourself a very important question— 'How well can I do this job?' Only if you are able to perform at or above your employer's expectations can you retain the job and flourish in it.

The job description helps you answer this question: 'Can I do this job with enthusiasm and very well every day?' If your honest answer to the above question is, 'No, I can't', then you should not apply for the job.

The second and most important question is: Based on my qualifications, personality and passion, which job description will suit me the most? This is covered in the later sections. Before we move further, let me just take a minute or two to re-emphasize the importance of taking a job in an area that you like, if not love.

The world is becoming competitive and everyone is looking for money, fame and recognition. If you want to be mediocre that is fine but if you want to be somebody of significance, you have to be very good at what you do.

In other words, if you want to fulfil your dreams in life, you have to be very good at what you do. And to be very good at what you do, you have to like the job that you do—imagine Sachin Tendulkar as a singer, Lata Mangeshkar as a banking executive, or M.S. Dhoni as a doctor; everyone cannot be good at everything. Each of us can do only certain things very well.

Finding the right job—why is it important?

Why is it important to find your RFJ? Because it is the foundation of your career. When you are building a house, experts will tell you that the foundation determines how big and how tall the building will be. In other words, you design the foundation based on how tall and big is the building you want to construct. Similarly, the first job should be chosen with care because it will determine how tall and big your career will be.

We have analyzed thousands of résumés of successful professionals in the corporate sector and found that more than educational qualifications, it is the first job that had a greater impact on their career. Most of the CEOs had a great start in their first job.

What happens if I join the wrong job?

Nine out of ten freshers take the first available job because they become desperate. Very soon, they start 'hating' that job and quit, moving on to the next available job. Again, they find the job very difficult, or very boring, and quit. So, if the first job is not the right job, they start off as rolling stones and their career becomes stunted. Many of them settle for a job that they dislike and every working day becomes a reason for suffering.

How do I know that I am in my RFJ?

Simple—when you get up in the morning, do you look forward to going to work? Are you learning something every day? Do you find your self-confidence growing? Do you find your boss and colleagues praising you for your hard work and positive attitude? If the answer to the above questions is 'yes', then you have arrived at your RFJ.

Let's now understand about the five aspects of the RFJ.

The five RFJ targets you need to meet

Meeting each of the following five targets impacts your success in a job, and your career progression thereafter. These targets are:

1. Finding the right job role,
2. in the right industry,
3. with the right employer,
4. at the right level, and
5. in the right city.

Why? Because let us take the example of one of India's celebrated CEOs, M.S. Banga. In 2000, Banga was elected Chairman and CEO of one of India's largest and most reputed companies the fast moving consumer goods (FMCG) companies—Hindustan Lever Ltd. (HLL, now renamed Hindustan Unilever Limited). At that time, he was the youngest CEO ever to be appointed as Chairman of HLL.

Banga joined HLL in Sales and Marketing as a management trainee at its Mumbai office. He identified and got the right job role (sales and marketing), in the right industry (FMCG), with the right employer (HLL), at the right level (management trainee), and in the right city (Mumbai). In other words, he met all five RFJ targets at one go when he joined HLL. This made him Chairman of HLL at the young age of forty-six.

So, what are these five targets all about? Well, the right role depends upon your personality and is extensively covered in Chapter 2. Choice of the right industry determines your career growth—both with and after the first employer—and is covered in Chapter 3. The first employer shapes your work ethics and how to choose the right employer is covered in Chapter 4. Entering the job at the right level is important and is covered in Chapter 5. How to choose the city for your RFJ is covered in Chapter 6.

It is important to plan and work towards meeting all five targets. In case your current job meets only a few components but not all five, don't worry; you are yet to find the RFJ and, hence, choose the next job based on the guidelines given here. But to find the RFJ, you must know about yourself first. To know yourself, you need to research about yourself.

Knowing yourself—The only way to meet your five RFJ targets

No one knows you better than you, and hence, you have to own this task. If needed, do some research on yourself!

How do you identify the five targets of RFJ? The easiest and most common way is to ask your senior at college, or seek the help of family members. Both these options (asking the senior or family members) have severe limitations. First, they have limited knowledge based on their own experience. Your family members have a limited number of friends, and the view of each family member is limited to his/her and their experiences.

Second, they often have an unrealistic opinion on what you should do. I have met several parents who wanted their child to do what they themselves could not do. In other words, they were not interested in what the child wanted to do but were more interested in their own dreams. Many children take up jobs that they hate because their parents pushed them. Similarly, your senior, too, can offer only limited advice. That is because no one knows you better than yourself.

The selection of the RFJ depends upon your personality, your desires, your dreams, etc., and you yourself know these best.

Researching yourself

Let me give you an example of why research helps. A year ago, I met Meena (name changed) who had joined an expensive course to become a flight attendant. At that time, the aviation industry was going through a very difficult time; employees were being downsized, salaries were not paid on time. The newspapers were full of articles on the aviation industry and its travails, but Meena, who never read the business section of the newspaper, ended up completing the course and not getting the flight attendant job.

Begin your research by:

- owning the task—that is, you need to do research about yourself;
- talking to your friends and reading about your role models;
- using the Internet to search for answers. Read the daily newspapers—especially the 'business' section— and business magazines which regularly carry articles on industrial growth and news on fast growing sectors and companies.

Finally, the selection of an RFJ is your responsibility; you can take advice from others but the decision has to be yours and only yours. A lot more detail on 'how to research' is covered in Chapter 4.

Once you identify the RFJ, then the task is to get it. To do that, you need to first understand how companies recruit.

How companies recruit

Employers conduct objective tests to eliminate and reduce the number of applicants, and then conduct subjective tests to select and recruit. You have to be good at both. The recruitment process followed by Indian companies for hiring freshers is more or less the same in all industries. Since you do not have work experience, companies will assess the following:

▫ who you are (your personality); and

▫ what you are good at (your skills).

There will be a different assessment process for different job roles. In case of technical jobs, you will have to take technical written tests; a few companies may also conduct a technical interview. Some companies insist on aptitude tests and so you must prepare yourself for that. Many companies prefer online aptitude and technical tests. So you need to be comfortable with online tests.

Group Discussions (GDs) are popular mainly in campus recruitments. If you are looking for a job outside the campus, GDs may not be conducted. Most companies will conduct an HR interview. Detailed tips on each of these important assessments discussed above are given in later chapters.

Many freshers believe that the fewer the assessments, the better their chances of getting a job. There is only partial truth in this argument. Some assessments, like the HR interview, are very subjective and, hence, it is entirely possible that good candidates may not be selected. This is very visible in campus interviews. Toppers are often rejected while mediocre candidates who communicate well are selected.

In my view, if you are good in your subjects and prepare properly, then you should prefer more objective assignments like aptitude and written tests, because you have a better chance of getting the job.

Broadly, the private sector companies use the aptitude/ technical tests and GD to eliminate and reduce the number of candidates for interview. So interviews, technical and HR, are the final and also most important assessments based on which the offer will be made.

But public sector undertakings (PSU's) and Government jobs give most weightage to written tests and lower weightage to interviews. So it is important to do these tests very well if you are looking for a job in a PSU or with the Government.

Typically, the private sector would want two candidates in the final interview for every vacancy. The ratio in PSU can vary from 1.5 to three candidates for every vacancy at the final interview stage.

Typically, a fresher should expect to attend 10–15 interviews before he/she gets the right first job. So do not get depressed if your first five or six interviews are not successful. Use every test or interview as a learning experience; analyze what went wrong and improve next time.

Let's talk a bit about what you must do after getting the RFJ—that is, career planning.

Career planning—Why is it important?

Many of you may have already taken up a wrong first job. Now, is there a possibility for you to still correct this mistake and take up the right job? The answer is YES. You can still make up and get into the right job. This aspect is covered extensively in Chapters 17 and 18 in this book, but here are a few career planning tips.

◻ **Don't panic just because your RFJ salary is not enough**
The RFJ that may come to you may not always give you the lifestyle that you desire. Then what do you do? You may have many commitments that you made in your personal life, so how do you manage all your commitments? The best option to improve your lifestyle is to improve your skills-set, get more incentives and become more productive. But do not change jobs just because you want a better salary.

◻ **Stay in the first job for a longer term**
If you want to succeed in life, the basic rule is to stay in

your right first job for a long term. By that, I mean, eight to ten years for non IT and five years for IT. According to our research, many CEOs acquired their position by spending long years in their RFJ. If you stick in the RFJ for a longer period, your career will pickup momentum and put you on the right trajectory.

◻ **Pace yourself**
Imagine that you are a part of a long race. Therefore, you need to always be yourself and pace yourself. You need not copy anyone. Just because he/she succeeded fast doesn't mean you also should try to copy them. Every individual is different and so is the skills-set. So work on improving your skills and, most importantly, believe in yourself.

2

YOUR PERSONALITY DETERMINES YOUR RIGHT FIRST JOB

What is 'personality'? People in this world belong to many personality types. For instance, let us look at two people: Lalu Prasad Yadav and Sachin Tendulkar. Both are Members of Parliament. While Laluji was a member of the Lok Sabha, Sachin was nominated to the Rajya Sabha. But both of them have different personalities. Lalu Yadav is very social and practical and is a great organiser, while Sachin is a focused, very disciplined but an introverted person. Who is a more successful politician? Clearly Laluji. Because of his personality. Why is Sachin such a great cricketer? Because of his personality.

Knowing your personality type

Students, whilst in their academic phase, are usually inclined towards learning and gathering knowledge about the external world in general and their domain subjects in particular. What is often missed out is self-awareness. However, knowing your personality—in other words, being self-aware about it—is the first step in finding the RFJ; it will help you choose the right career and the right job. It will also help you become more efficient, as you start accepting yourself as you are and try to develop your skills.

Only when 'self-knowledge' is used to make decisions and predict one's own behaviour in various contexts, can we call it real self-awareness. Thus, while life experiences help in shaping one's personality and preferences, real wisdom lies in being able to harness this knowledge towards building one's future.

By knowing your personality, you get to know your strengths, work on them and become more productive. You also get to identify what your weak areas are so that you can work towards improving yourself.

Freshers sometimes get confused with what exactly they want to do, because there are many choices available in today's world. So if you know your personality, it will help you identify what career option is best for you. When you know what is good for you, it boosts your self-confidence. When you know what you want, you can be more confident while attending interviews or giving tests. Let us look at some more important aspects of personality assessments.

Personality testing

Self-awareness is about knowing your strengths and weaknesses, among other things. Awareness of these helps you to use or work upon them to continuously grow and improve. Self-awareness is a continuous and never-ending process.

Personality testing is the field of study concerned with the theory and technique of psychological measurement, which includes the measurement of attitudes and personality traits. Using psychometrics we can analyze the fitment—between the job role and personality type.

Dr John Holland's 'Theory of Careers'—An ideal way to test the personality of freshers

Well-known psychologist Dr John Holland developed a psychometric test in the 1970s that can help in understanding the personality and its relationship with careers. This test is called John Holland's 'Theory of Careers' and Dr Holland proposed that people work best in work environments that match their preferences.

The 'Theory of Careers' identifies your personality type and the roles suitable to your personality, and is based on the theory of 'birds of the same feather flock together'. In a simple sense, it means 'people with similar personalities tend to work together'. This 'Theory of Careers' is the basis for most of the career inventories used today. It is supported by 500 research studies worldwide and used by over 22 million people worldwide. It has also been translated into twenty-five different languages.

What is my personality as per Dr Holland's theory? Am I Realistic because I don't daydream, or am I Investigative because it's always me who smells the rat first? I am good at drawing, so does it mean I am Artistic? I am on Facebook, so does it mean I am Social? Perhaps I am more Enterprising as I have great dreams of being a CEO of a company. I keep a record of my expenses, does that mean I am Conventional?

Often, we make such assumptions about our personality type. Having a perspective is definitely a good idea, but a personality test is a more scientific way of discovering our most dominating personality traits.

Six personality dimensions: John Holland

According to research by John Holland and others, each personality is made up of six personality dimensions—Realistic

(R), Investigative (I), Artistic (A), Social (S), Enterprising (E), and Conventional (C) —RIASEC, in short. Though elaborated further in the next chapter, I would like to touch upon them briefly here.

Realistic people are more practical who like to invest their time working with tangible things like machines, tools, etc.

Investigative people are more into problem solving or analytical work. They enjoy intellectual work like studying science or solving maths problems.

Artistic people love creative arts like dance, music, painting, etc. They are very expressive and original.

Social people have a helpful nature and are people-oriented. They have a very friendly and empathetic nature.

Enterprising people are more 'selling' type personalities, very persuasive in nature. They are ambitious people with a never-say-die attitude.

Conventional people are very organized and systematic. They like discipline and following standard rules or procedures.

If you want to learn more about the common traits and preferences of each of the six personality traits (dimensions), you could refer to the following tables.

In John Holland's tests, you get scores against each of the six dimensions—low scores in some dimensions and high scores in some. This combination of scores is called a personality type.

Let us see, for example, what Sachin Tendulkar's scores are likely to be (if he takes the John Holland test)—high scores on the Realistic, Artistic and Conventional dimensions, and medium scores in the Enterprising, Social and Investigative dimensions. In the case of Lalu Prasad Yadav, the former chief minister of Bihar, the scores are likely to be high on the Social, Realistic and

Common Traits of Each Personality Type

Realistic	Investigative	Artistic	Social	Enterprising	Conventional
Hard-headed, inflexible, persistent, nature lover, curious about the physical world, mechanically inclined, materialistic, straightforward/ frank, genuine, concrete, systematic, stable, reserved, self-controlled, independent, athletic, thrifty, ambitious	Analytical, intellectual, scholarly, scientific, observant, logical, precise, curious, inquisitive, independent, intellectually self-confident, complex, broad-minded, pessimistic, reserved	Idealistic, unconventional, impractical, complicated, creative, intuitive, imaginative, original, innovative, introspective, sensitive, emotional, impulsive, expressive, open, nonconformist, independent, courageous	Generous, kind, forgiving, patient, friendly, understanding, helpful, sensitive, cooperative, tactful, persuasive, emphatic, responsible, insightful, outgoing	Extroverted, adventurous, enthusiastic, energetic, optimistic, ambitious, agreeable, sociable, self-confident, assertive, persuasive, popular, exhibitionist, talkative, impulsive, spontaneous, inquisitive	Efficient, conscientious, inflexible, methodical, systematic, structured, well-organized, orderly, conforming, obedient, accurate, polite, numerically inclined, practical, ambitious, thrifty, persistent, defensive

Common Traits of Each Personality Type

Realistic	Investigative	Artistic	Social	Enterprising	Conventional
Working outdoors	Exploring a variety of ideas	Attending concerts, theatre, art exhibition	Working in groups/ leading group discussions	Making decisions that affect others	Following clearly defined procedures
Hands-on mechanical work	Working independently	Working on crafts	Participating in meetings	Playing a leading role	Working with numbers
Being physically active	Reading scientific or technical journals	Expressing self creatively	Working with young people	Starting own service or business	Being responsible for details
Building things	Dealing with abstractions/ abstract thinking	Reading fiction, plays and poetry	Serving others	Meeting important people	Using gadgets
Training animals	Being challenged	Taking photographs	Expressing clearly	Standing for elections	Becoming a typist/taking shorthand

Common Traits of Each Personality Type

Realistic	Investigative	Artistic	Social	Enterprising	Conventional
Working on electronic equipment	Solving maths problems and complex calculations	Dealing with ambiguous ideas	Mediating disputes and cooperating with others	Selling activities	Collecting or organizing things
Playing sports	Gaming, solving puzzles		Helping people with problems	Campaigning politically	
	Using computers and gadgets, programming		Doing volunteer work	Seeking positions of power	
	Performing lab experiments		Playing team sports		
	Analyzing data, doing research		Teaching/ training others		
	Understanding scientific theories		Planning and supervising an activity		

Enterprising dimensions, and medium or low in the Investigative, Artistic and Conventional dimensions. This may explain why Sachin and Laluji are two different personality types.

Adapting the John Holland test to the Indian context

Though the John Holland test has been used the world over, modifications needed to be made to the test to fit the Indian context. The vocabulary used in the test required changes. The TMI Group, in association with a leading professor from XLRI, Jamshedpur (a leading educational institution of India), adapted this test for Indian conditions, and we have subsequently used the test for thousands of fresh candidates in India.

The four types of work environment

Just as every human being has a personality type, every job role has a certain work environment. When you choose a job role which has a work environment that matches your personality type, your chance of success is very high. This is the secret of success of many a corporate sector CEO. The first step in this process is to understand the four types of work environments.

- Sales Work Environment
- Support Work Environment
- Process Work Environment
- Developer Work Environment

There are plenty of jobs a fresher can do. These jobs are across many functions like HR, finance, marketing, sales, manufacturing, operations, IT, legal, etc., and across many industries. It is very important to note that in each different function and in each industry, there are specific job roles with the above four different work environments. For example, even in the manufacturing function, there are roles with 'sales type' work environments.

Understanding 'sales' type work environment

Typical sales work environments require a person to sell products or services, or concepts or ideas. The customers could be individuals or organizations. They could be external or internal to an organization. So sales type work environments are not limited to the sales department alone; they exist in all the other departments like HR; etc., too. To succeed in the sales work environment, you require the following behavioural traits—high tolerance for ambiguity, extroversion, ambitious, persuasive, friendly, and expressive.

Examples of sales type work environments would be direct sales roles like selling water purifiers, outbound calling jobs in call centres, corporate communications, etc.

Understanding 'support' type work environment

Support work environments require the following behavioural traits—helpful, problem solving oriented, analytical thinking, self-control, persistent, concern for others, adaptability/flexibility, independent thinking, systematic, inward looking and persuasive.

Examples of support work environments include systems integration roles in IT, technical support roles in BPO, engineering supervisor role in manufacturing, etc.

Understanding 'process' type work environment

Process work environments require the following behavioural traits—dealing with the routine, eye for detail, stay within prescribed limits, systematic approach, practical, stick to established path, low/moderate need for 'outside the office' activities, low/moderate need to involve with people, strong urge to conform, comfortable in activities involving computers/

machines/ processes, low need for variety, low tolerance for ambiguity and change.

Examples of process work environments include training roles in HR, network operations roles in IT, production supervisor role in manufacturing, etc.

Understanding 'developer' type work environment

Developer work environments require the following behavioural traits: creativity, innovation, original thinking, questioning and analysis, expressive, curious, intellectually self-confident, persistent, independent.

Examples of developer type work environments include web design in IT, R&D roles in manufacturing, management consulting roles, etc.

The table below establishes the fact that there are many roles across functions and across industries in each type of work environment.

Table: Examples of roles in the four types of work environments

Industry	Sales WE	Support WE	Process WE	Developer WE
IT	Outbound call executive	Inbound call centre executive	GIS executive	Process Trasitionist
Banking	CASA executive	Recovery officer	Probationary officer	Treasury executive
Manufacturing	Vendor development executive	Production shift in charge	Quality control executive	Product designer

Healthcare (hospitals)	Patient care executive	Equipment maintenance executive	Pharmacy assistant	Emergency technician
Hospitality	Banquet sales	Front office executive	House keeping executive	Chef
Entertainment	Marketing executive	Production executive	Film editor	Film director
Advertising	Client servicing executive	Media planning executive	Media operations	Copywriter

Table: Examples of job roles with different work environments (WE) across functions

Function	Sales WE	Support WE	Process WE	Developer WE
Finance	Fund raising	Accounting	Audit	Treasury
HR	Recruiter	Employee relations	Training coordination	Corporate HR
IT	Key account management	Network management	Code testing	Product architect
Operations	Construction supervision	Production	Logistics	Process improvement
Legal	Partner-in-law firm	Solicitor	Patent analyst	Trial lawyer

Now that you have an idea of your personality type and also understand the types of work environment, the next step is to match your personality type with the work environment type.

Selecting the right job role matching your personality

Everyone has a different personality and, therefore, different likes and dislikes, and everybody has different things that make them happy. In the same context, everyone, depending on their personality, has different roles that naturally suit them.

The John Holland theory goes a step beyond describing personality types and links it to career choices. People of the same personality tend to 'flock together'. People of the same personality type work together in a job and create a work environment that fits their type. How you act and feel at work depends on your workplace environment type to a large extent. People who choose to work in an environment similar to their personality type are more likely to be successful and satisfied.

Primary and secondary personality

Based on your scores in RIASEC dimensions in the John Holland's test modified to Indian context, you can determine the primary and secondary work environments that will suit your personality.

Primary work environment is the work environment closest to your personality, and the secondary environment is the second work environment closest to your personality.

As discussed earlier, there are job roles in every function and every industry in each of the four work environment types. So, while your educational qualification could determine the function and industry that you may wish to join, you can identify job roles that suit the work environment designed for your personality.

For example, an engineer could have a sales profile and actually turn out to be a good salesperson in the manufacturing industry. Similarly, an engineer could have a developer personality and become a great advertising professional.

Let's now understand the problems in doing a job which does

not suit your personality. If you are a creative person with a BCom degree and you become an audit assistant which is a repetitive job, you will either get bored or quit, or you will continue in the nine-to-five job and look for other avenues for expression. You will be substandard, mediocre and unhappy even if you manage to acquire ICWA or CA qualifications. Therefore, it is essential that you find a role that suits your personality type.

Twelve possible job personality types

Twelve combinations exist based on the primary and secondary work environments, as given below.

Category	Primary Work Environment	Secondary Work Environment	Sample roles for this personality type
1	Sales	Support	Corporate communications
2	Sales	Process	Voice call centre—Outbound calls
3	Sales	Developer	Concept selling
4	Support	Sales	Investor relations
5	Support	Process	Voice call centre—Inbound calls
6	Support	Developer	Tech support
7	Process	Sales	Circulations dept in a newspaper
8	Process	Support	Airport security
9	Process	Developer	Stunt coordinator in film industry

Category	Primary Work Environment	Secondary Work Environment	Sample roles for this personality type
10	Developer	Sales	Copywriting in advertising
11	Developer	Support	Crime detective
12	Developer	Process	Graphic designing

These twelve categories above are referred to as 'Job Personality Type' in this book. There is a four-step process to determine the right job role fitting your personality.

Step 1: Find out your RIASEC score based on John Holland's test.

Step 2: Using these scores, determine the work environment—primary and secondary—that will suit your personality.

Step 3: Career preference—identify job roles fitting your primary and secondary work environment categories.

Step 4: Select from these job roles those that gives you a natural advantage based on your qualifications.

JP Fit Test—A way to find the right role for your RFJ

We have discussed extensively about the guidelines for finding a job that fits your personality in the earlier chapters. Is there an automated test which does this? If so, how can you access this?

The TMI group has developed a computerized test called JP Fit (Job Personality Fitment) test. This test is available online at http://www.tmie2eacademy.com/JPFitTest/Registration.aspx

JP Fit is a proprietary, pen and paper test developed by the TMI group. It consists of a table where there are twenty-five rows each containing six adjectives. You have to go through each row and allocate 10 points among the TOP THREE ADJECTIVES that describe you as a person. Of course, the word that describes you the best in that row, gets the highest number of points; then the next best word; and then the third best, and so on. Don't give points in decimals (for example 2.5; 3.7, etc.), give yourself points like 2, 7, 9, etc. You should be able to finish the test in approximately 10 minutes. Please note that there are no right or wrong answers. So you need to be honest while answering.

The TMI Group, based on its experience of hiring over 1,00,000 executives and managers, has developed an algorithm whereby the RIASEC scores are first arrived at and subsequently converted, by a computer program, into your two dominating personality categories—primary and secondary—that will determine your RFJ.

Why is JP Fit useful for freshers?

It is informative and not only focuses on giving you the personality report but it also tries to educate you about the basics of each personality dimension.

It is also user-friendly because it is simple and easy to understand and very easy to take.

It is specially designed for a fresher with very basic or no knowledge about the job market.

The JP Fit report

The JP Fit report is exhaustive and contains six sections. In Section 1, the report introduces the psychometric test and the basis for the JP Fit test. Section 2 explains the concept of work environment groupings and introduces the four work environment groupings. Section 3 covers the details of John Holland test. Section 4 is about your personal scores and their interpretation. It recommends your primary and secondary personality. Section 5 is about how interviewers can use the findings of the test. Section 6 is about how you—the test-taker—should use this report.

Effectiveness of JP Fit

The TMI group conducted a validation test among insurance sales managers and found there was a 95 per cent correlation between the test recommendation and the actual job performance of the managers. The study found that 95 per cent of the successful managers were personalities that fit 'sales' as their primary or secondary job groups.

In summary, the JP Fit test will guide you with a list of RFJ—please note that there may be many RFJs for each person.

3

FINDING THE RIGHT INDUSTRY
FOR THE RIGHT FIRST JOB

Types of industries

If you want to get the right first job (RFJ) to kick-start your career, you need to be in an industry that is right for you. But before looking at the various types of industries and finding one that suits you, let us look at what an industry is.

An industry is a place where production of products/services occurs. Industries in India play a major role in developing the economy as well as providing employment opportunities to people from both urban and rural areas. At the beginning of the twentieth century, India was a land of agriculture on a large scale. But with changing times, the country has evolved tremendously, giving birth to various industries that produce and deliver a variety of goods/products and services.

An industry can be classified into two types, based on the manpower requirements, production capacity and cost of inception:

□ micro-, small- and medium-scale industries (MSME's); and

□ large-scale industries.

According to the MSME Development Act of 2006, MSME industries can be classified as micro, small and medium, based on their investment requirements.

Classification of industries	Manufacturing/ production enterprises (investment limit)	Service enterprises (investment limit)
Micro	₹25 lakh	₹10 lakh
Small	₹5 crores	₹2 crores
Medium	₹10 crores	₹5 crores

Large-scale industries or heavy industries are those which require much higher investments, heavy manpower and machinery, and also employ a larger number of people.

There are various types of industries in our country. They can be differentiated according to the products they produce and services they provide. Central Statistical Organisation, Government of India, has published a National Industrial Classification (2008) of all economic activities into nineteen broad headings (http://mospi.nic.in/Mospi_New/site/inner.aspx?status=2&menu_id=129)

From the viewpoint of graduate jobs, National Skill Development Corporation (NSDC) has created thirty-two sector skill councils to cover the various industries in manufacturing, service and IT, as given below.

Sl no	Industry Sector	Sl no	Industry Sector	Sl no	Industry Sector
1	Aerospace and aviation	12	Gems and jewellery	23	Mining
2	Agriculture	13	Handicrafts and carpets	24	Plumbing

3	Apparel	14	Heath care	25	Power
4	Automotive	15	Hydrocarbon	26	Retail
5	Banking, financial services and insurance	16	Iron and steel	27	Rubber
6	Beauty and wellness	17	IT and ITeS	28	Security
7	Capital goods	18	Leather	29	Sports, physical education, fitness
8	Construction	19	Life sciences	30	Telecom
9	Earth moving and infrastructure building equipment	20	Logistics	31	Textile and handloom
10	Electronics	21	Management and management services	32	Tourism and hospitality
11	Food	22	Media and entertainment		

Every industry comes with its own HR policies and employment practices. What a prospective employee should look for, while taking up a job in an industry, are the following.

◻ **Industry growth**: The most important aspect is to ascertain the growth prospects of the industry. For example, the IT industry was one of the highest growing industries in early 2000. Today, growth has declined significantly. Similarly, the telecom industry was growing exponentially when the sector was privatized. Today, the industry is going through difficult times and growth is very slow.

In 2013–14, the industry that is growing the fastest is the banking industry—with a lot of new banking licences being issued.

□ **Employment stability**: Some industries are glamorous from the outside. Salaries are attractive and designations are great. But are the jobs secure? Can you perform and sustain the job? Is there a trend of 'hire and fire'? Are the performance expectations realistic? These questions need to be answered. For example, the construction industry has a high 'churn rate' (people join and quit quickly) because the expectations are unrealistic.

□ **Work culture**: What kind of work culture is prevalent in this industry? Is it professional? Is it promoter driven? Professionals like to work in a professionally managed environment. For example, hospitals (health care) and construction industries are very promoter driven and professional management is quite rare.

□ **Worklife balance**: What sort of lifestyle will you have if you choose a particular industry. For example, if you take up a job in IT, then you may have to work against strict deadlines and, so therefore, you will have very limited time to spare for your family. So you need to make the right choice by deciding how much time you are willing to spend on your work and how much time you want to give your family.

□ **Compensation**: What is the money/compensation that you will get if you take up a job today in that particular industry? More importantly, what will you get after ten years of working in that industry? This directly depends on how well the industry is performing.

Understanding long-term industry trends

While looking at the above employment dimensions of any industry, you have to assess today's situation but, more importantly, make an assessment of what will be the situation ten years from now. Because you are planning a career in this industry, long-term trends are very important.

The table below gives you an idea of the employment dimensions of a few selected industries. Please note that this assessment is based on the current scenario and may change in the future.

Factors→	Industry growth prospects	Employment stability	Work culture	Work–life balance	Compen-sation
Industries↓					
IT	Moderate	Medium	Professional	Tough	High
Manufac-turing	Moderate	High	Partly professional	Balanced	Average
Education	High	High	Not professional	High	Below average
Airline	Medium	Low	Professional	Low	High
Banking	High	Medium	Professional	High	Moderate
Hospitality/ hotel	High	Medium	Professional	Low	Medium
Health-care	Medium	High	Not professional	High	Average

You will notice that every industry has its pros and cons. So you need to choose what is acceptable to you.

How to select the right industry for you

There are various industries available today, offering immense employment opportunities. Every industry is unique and has a different way of functioning. So how do you choose the right industry?

Choosing the right industry depends on your basic objective of life: what do you want to achieve in life? What matters most to you—money, power, or status? Twenty-five years from now, say when you are fifty years old, when you look back at your past, three things can happen:

- you feel on top of the world—you have reached the top in your profession, but your family life and health has suffered a lot;

- your achievement has been moderate but you feel that you missed the excitement of life; and

- your work achievement has been low, but you have been true to yourself and not compromised on what is important to you. You have grown spiritually. You have contributed to the growth of many people around you. Many people love you, including your children. But, financially, you are dependent on your children. Your savings have been low and you are unhappy about this.

So these are the many dimensions to success in life—money, power, health, peace of mind, family relationships, contribution to society, spiritual growth, etc. You cannot get everything and must decide what you are not willing to lose—what I call the 'price' of achievement. Select the industry and RFJ where the 'price' that you pay is acceptable to you.

4

CHOOSING THE RIGHT FIRST EMPLOYER

What can you expect from your first employer?

The first job is an extension of your education, because when you complete your education, you know 'how to write an exam' or even 'how to communicate', but you do not know 'how to work.'

You learn about professional work ethics in your first job. Your first employer provides the 'classroom' for your learning, and your first boss is your 'guru'. So your approach to your first job should be based on the above philosophy.

Any good employer will provide the following to a fresher.

Role induction

It's every employee's right to be inducted/ trained for the job role. Some companies provide exhaustive induction. But the majority of companies provide limited induction training. So you have to get the best out of this limited induction.

Performance expectation

You should expect the employer to tell you about how your performance will be measured. The Key Result Areas (KRAs) and Key Performance Indices (KPIs) must be explained to you.

Resource allocation

Your employer must provide you with basic resources to do your job. If you need a computer/laptop, the employer must provide this. If your job requires extensive travelling within the city, you can expect the employer to help you get a vehicle loan, and pay the petrol and maintenance costs for official travel. You should be reimbursed travel and board and lodging costs if you travel out of town.

Opportunity to learn and contribute

Your employer should give you opportunities to learn and contribute. Surely it will stretch your time and you must be prepared for it. For example, the company may conduct 'computer classes' on 'advanced Excel programming'. You should be allowed to participate, but the classes may be held on a holiday, so you have to forego the holiday and stretch yourself.

Similarly, if you are willing to be part of a special task force—as an understudy and help, then the employer should welcome you to contribute, provided you also perform in your assigned job.

No penalty for mistakes

When you do the job for the first time, you cannot get it right and you will make mistakes. The employer should not penalize you for that. It is important to realize the difference between mistakes and carelessness. No employer will tolerate carelessness. Even mistakes cannot be repeated and you must learn from them.

Challenging and strict targets

Your first job is the foundation of your career, and hence, expect it to be the 'toughest'. Super career performers always succeed because their first job was demanding and challenging. You are also young and energetic, and hence, you can put in extra-long hours at work. You are also expected to do many things at the same time (multi-tasking). Once you succeed at your first tough job, all subsequent jobs appear to be easy.

A good example is the Indian Army. After training, an officer is put into tough environments and expected to take on big challenges as a lieutenant or captain. Long hours at work are very common. This toughens the officer for his/her career success in the army.

What you cannot expect from your first employer

A nine-to-five job

Such jobs exist only in the Government service. Even there, things are changing. In the private sector, it is a minimum of twelve hours daily, six days a week. Be prepared. Therefore, stay close to your workplace so that travel time is minimal.

High compensation

If you are a learner, shouldn't you pay? In college, you paid the fees. So whatever the employer pays, receive it as a gift or bonus. You can expect your employer to pay a 'fair' salary proportionate to your contribution. As a learner, your contribution is limited and so the salary will be limited—to cover your living expenses. Do not expect the first employer to pay for your lavish lifestyle— pubs, partying, etc. If you get high salaries, be prepared that your employer will expect high services in return. If you do not achieve the given targets, you may lose the job.

So my advice is, expect a basic salary of ₹10,000 to ₹15,000 if you are a graduate (BA/BSc/BTech); and a basic of ₹15,000 to ₹20,000 if you are an MBA (with some knowledge of management). Beyond this, it is a bonus.

Instant growth

Many MBAs and graduates feel that they deserve a promotion because 'others' in the department are getting promoted. Growth will come later. Focus initially on learning and excelling in the job. In fact, if you get promoted, your responsibility and targets will grow and you may not be ready for the higher role. In my world, 'slow and steady' wins the race.

Pampering/mentoring

The employer and your boss have many more things to do than 'managing' you. You have to function on your own and take the initiative. Don't hang around in the corner and wait for people to invite you to participate. Very few organizations 'mentor' fresh employees; for example, the Big Five consulting companies have a 'mentor' for every fresh employee. But this is very rare and a huge bonus.

What can your first employer expect from you?

Right from the security guard level to a project manager at the top level, every employee is hired by the company so that he/she contributes much more than the salary. Each and every employee in the company is responsible for its effective functioning. Therefore, when an employer hires you by giving you a competitive pay package, the organization also has certain basic expectations from you.

It is very important that you understand what your employer is expecting from you at the interview stage itself, as it will be easier for you to prepare yourself. So when you get positive vibes during an interview about clinching the job, you must always ask your prospective employer their expectations. There is a basic set of expectations that every employer has from an employee. We discuss a few key expectations below.

Value for money

Every employee should contribute more than the salary. How much more varies depending upon the job role. Typically, the company incurs costs, in addition to your salary, which are called direct overheads. For example, the rent of the office space you occupy, the rentals of the computer/laptop you use, the electricity/ air conditioning, internet bandwidth, your boss's time, etc., are all part of what is called 'direct overheads'. On top of this, the company expects to recover indirect overheads—like the cost of the HR and Finance team, interest costs, etc.

So typically, the overall cost—salary + direct overheads or indirect overheads—at the entry level could be three to four times the salary paid to you. The employer will expect a surplus on top of all the above costs. So for an entry-level person, if you contribute five to six times the salary you earn, then you are a winner. If you are earning ₹15,000 per month, then your contribution should be ₹1 lakh per month.

The next question is how to measure contribution? In sales jobs, the profit/contribution of the business you bring in is the measure. If you are in finance, the savings in cost that you bring in is the measure. Therefore, one of the key questions to ask a potential employer during an interview is: 'How will my contribution be measured?'

The right attitude

Someone rightly said that 'your attitude determines your altitude'. Yes, it is very important that you have the right attitude towards your work and the job, because it will directly affect your relationship with your fellow workers, top management and also your deliverables.

What is the right attitude? Right attitude means positive attitude, contributing mindset (ask how you can add value and contribute before asking how you will benefit). Right attitude also means winning attitude ('never say die', and 'together, anything is possible'). It also means ownership ('I will behave as if I own this company till my last working day; I will not waste company resources'). It entails an inclusive mindset ('How can I work with you?' is the right question, and 'Why should I work with you?' is the wrong question), and compliance mindset ('How can I adhere to the office rules and regulations?' is the right question to ask, and 'Why should I follow the office rules and regulations?' is the wrong question).

During the interview, employers try to assess whether you have the 'right' attitude for the job and, hence, it pays to communicate the 'right' attitude that you have.

Reliability

Rahul Dravid is called Mr Dependable and the 'Wall of Indian Cricket'. Why? It is because of his consistent performance and scoring rate. He has always delivered whenever the country needed him to score runs and play a good game of cricket.

In the same way, organizations also look for reliable people. When your superior hands over a task to you, he/she expects that you will complete the task within the specified time-frame, helping them to achieve deadlines.

Learner's attitude

When an employee makes an effort to learn new aspects at work and upgrade his/her skills, he/she always impresses the boss. What do I mean by learner's attitude? To begin with, your attitude should be: 'I don't know', which will keep your mind open to learning. Second, you should be inquisitive: How does this work? Is there a better way of doing this? Third, you should search and read a lot on the internet: Study how others are doing the same task that you are doing. What are the best practices?

The key to learning is asking questions, and seeking answers to these questions sincerely. Lastly a learner's mindset includes 'learning by doing'. Unless you try and do, your learning is only 'textbook learning'. Experimenting on different ways of doing is a big step.

Taking the initiative and being friendly

Bosses like people who come forward and take the initiative to complete a task/work. It helps in creating the right impression as well as it improves your skills since you get to work on new projects.

Working in a team

Teamwork is often important for the overall success of a project. Imagine if the players in the Indian Cricket Team did not get along well with each other, what would happen? It will directly affect the performance of the team. Therefore, you must be a team player and maintain cordial relations with your superiors and co-workers.

Loyalty and confidentiality

When you are working for an organization, you must ensure that you are loyal to your paymaster and see that no confidential information goes out from the organization. When an organization hires you, it expects you to maintain secrecy and confidentiality of important information.

Four dimensions of employer positioning

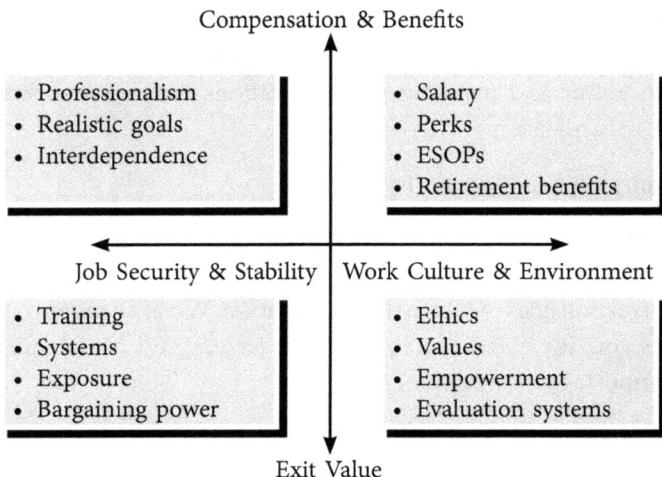

Every employer is different. Each one has a different way of working, in terms of culture, compensation and benefits policy, etc. Keeping this in mind, the TMI Group has set up a proprietary framework known as GEP (Good Employer Proposition), which is a blend of multiple factors like work culture, growth potential, reward and recognition, salary, etc.

Employers/organizations can be of different sizes such as multinational companies, Indian companies, medium-sized companies, small-sized companies and micro companies, based on their investment. Each of these organizations has a unique strategy for recruiting employees.

Th erefore, with multiple choices available today, candidates also have to take a decision regarding which employer they want to work for. Here, the GEP helps candidates zero in on potential employers. Th e GEP has four dimensions, as shown below.

FOUR DIMENSIONS OF EMPLOYER POSITIONING

Compensation & Benefits

- Professionalism
- Realistic goals
- Interdependence

- Salary
- Perks
- ESOPs
- Retirement benefits

Job Security & Stability | Work Culture & Environment

- Training
- Systems
- Exposure
- Bargaining power

- Ethics
- Values
- Empowerment
- Evaluation systems

Exit Value

Compensation and benefits

This includes the salary offered and the other benefits of working in the organization. Benefits refer to long- and short-term benefits, including conveyance, leave travel, medical and retirement benefits.

Job security

How well is the organization and the industry performing? Is the job safe? Does the company follow a 'hire and fire' policy? Is the company paying salaries on time? These are some of the questions that you need to ask.

Work culture

What are the organizational values, vision, mission and goals, and how is the organization working towards achieving the same? How does it treat its employees? Is there a professional atmosphere? Are the targets realistic? Is the decision-making decentralized? Is there a performance management system in place? These are some of the questions that you need to ask.

Exit value

How are you benefited when you exit the company? What will be your market value when you decide to exit? Will the company give you an opportunity to learn 'rare' and 'in-demand' skills? Will the company train you to become a 'complete' professional? What are the promotion avenues within the company and within the group (if the company is part of a group like the TATAs)? These are some of the questions that you need to ask.

Choosing the right first employer

The GEP framework tells you how every employer is unique. No employer offers you the best in all the four dimensions— compensation, exit value, work culture and employment stability. For example, TATA group of companies offers excellent job security and work culture but moderate (medium) salary and moderate exit value. Private sector companies offer excellent work culture and better compensation but moderate (medium) job security and low exit value. The work culture in PSUs is more bureaucratic (low in work culture) but provides high job security. So every employer is different. You need to choose what you want.

My advice on choosing the first employer

My advice is to choose the first employer who offers moderate (medium) compensation, but provides excellent (high) exit value because of the training and learning opportunities and growth prospects within the company; has a very professional work culture (high on work culture dimension); does not guarantee a job for life but insists on performance to retain the job (medium on job security dimension). This combination is what I would choose for myself.

How to research your employer?

Having discussed what to look for in the right first employer, we need to address the next question: How do I research or find out the real truth about the employer?

There is no simple or easy way to find out the full truth. To begin with, you must expect the employer to tell you only what the employer wants you to know. So the truth has to be found out by researching/talking to people.

Here are some of the ways to find out the truth.

▫ Search on Google News—all the press coverage about the employer will be there in the Google News section.

▫ Talk to recruitment consultants, who keep tabs on employers and have reliable and correct information—provided you are able to extract it from them.

▫ Talk to college alumni—your college alumni (your seniors) may know someone working in that company.

▫ Talk to employees or ex-employees. Find out a way to reach an employee/ex-employee of the company—some relative of yours may know them.

▫ Study the leadership team profile. If the leadership team has a highly qualified and professional background, it is a good indicator.

▫ Ask for feedback about the company—on social websites like LinkedIn or community websites.

▫ Read business newspapers and business magazines regularly.

5

THE BEST ENTRY LEVEL
IN THE RIGHT FIRST JOB

Should you join as a manager or a trainee?

In our country, people are very concerned about what designation they are given when they join a company. For many, it is a matter of pride to be called a team lead/manager.

But have you asked yourself if you are really ready to be a manager or team lead? Employers may offer you these designations/positions to lure you or retain you in the company. But the fact is, as a fresher, you are not ready for taking up managerial roles as you are new to the industry, company and the job profile.

When you join a company, your temperament should be that of a learner/trainee. When you join as a trainee, expectations from you as an employee are not very high. Since very little is expected from you, you can exceed expectations and earn the goodwill of your boss.

You must always treat the first two years of your job as an extension of your education. You will be able to learn the maximum and get a grip on all the necessary work processes during these two years. If you learn to handle all the details of the job—no matter how small or insignificant—competently, you become more confident, are able to understand the job role organizational values, and the employer's expectations from you. As you continue to work in this manner towards excelling in your job, you will definitely reap benefits in the long run.

Position/ level	Employer expecta- tions	Stress levels	Learning	Targets	Risk	Salary
Trainee/ analyst	Low	Low	High	Minimum	Low	Low
Executive/ Senior analyst	Moderate	Moderate	High	Moderate	Medium	Medium
Manager	High	High	Low	Very high	High	High

The above table gives you the pros and cons of accepting a trainee role or a managerial role. So joining as a trainee in your right first job is always more beneficial than joining at higher levels.

Working as an executive/manager in the RFJ

Once you look at the table above, you will understand that joining directly in managerial positions, without prior experience, calls for a lot of risk even though the pay may be high. In addition to the above, there are two other dimensions—managing people and a wider job role.

Who is a manager?

A manager is a person who is responsible for managing the productivity, targets, learning and growth of one or more individuals reporting to him/her, in addition to meeting his/her own targets. A manager is expected to know the workflow and process involved in a particular role.

For example, if you are an HR Manager, you may be managing a team of recruitment executives, performance management executives, compensation and benefits executives, employee engagement executives and staffing executives. Without prior experience, you will not know the best way to manage all these people, and so, you may miss out on deadlines/targets. This will lead to lots of issues and you may be fired from your job. But if you join as an HR Trainee or an HR Executive, you get to know/learn how the whole HR department functions. As days go by, you will become more and more confident and will gain maximum knowledge about the workflow.

Therefore, it is always good for a fresher to take up trainee/ executive positions than directly join as a manager.

Entrepreneur and manager

All entrepreneurs have to do many roles and often do managerial jobs. So, if you are a fresher and want to be an entrepreneur, it is similar to accepting a managerial role without any experience. My advice is not to start an entrepreneurial venture until you have worked in a professional organization, learnt how to work and also learnt how to get work out of others.

6

CHOOSING THE CITY
FOR YOUR RIGHT FIRST JOB

Looking for a job outside your home-town

Before looking for that right first job (RFJ), the first thing you must think about is whether you want to work from your home-town or work outside your home-town, and also about overseas opportunities. It is extremely important to be clear about 'how prepared you are?' to work outside your home-town.

If you are applying for a job within your home-town, there is not much to think about because you can continue living in the same house with your parents. But if you are applying for a job in a different location, then there are various factors that you need to consider. Let us look at some of them.

Factors that one needs to think about if working outside your home-town:

Finances

First and foremost, you need to analyze if your family's and your financial condition permit you to work from a different location. You need to think about how you are going to manage your stay (rent), food, travel, other expenses, etc.

Place of stay

One of the most important and crucial factors that you need to consider is your place of stay in a different location. Let us assume that your home town is Hyderabad but your work location is in Bengaluru. Then, you need to think about a place for you to stay in Bengaluru (whether it will be a working men/women's hostel, or a relative's house, or you yourself want to take a house on rent, or your company itself is providing you with some accommodation). Generally, for girls in our country, it is a really tough decision to make because parents are worried about the safety of their child.

Food

This is another important factor. If you are staying in a hostel or a relative's house, you need not worry about food. But if you take a place on rent and stay on your own, it might be a challenge if you do not know how to cook. Then, you might have to eat outside daily, which is not a very good option as it will affect your finances and health, or you might have to employ a cook who will cook food for you (this also will take a toll on your finances), or learn to cook yourself.

The daily commute

Commuting in a different city can also be a challenge till you become familiar with the place or make new friends who can guide you about the best means of commuting in the city. You may also need a vehicle (two-wheeler). Can you afford to buy a two-wheeler? How far is the place of work from your home? Is public transport available? How much time will be spent on the daily commute? These are some questions you need to ask.

Savings

Work out how much you will save—after all expenses. Work out how to cut the cost of living so that you can save, because you may not want to ask your parents for money after being employed. Even in expensive cities such as Mumbai and Delhi, it is possible to live frugally and save money—provided you plan.

Last year, a young girl named Priya (name changed) came to me looking for a job. Her problem was that her ₹50,000 per month (take home) salary was not enough to support her lifestyle, which included partying and eating out regularly. She wanted to earn more, so took up another job with a higher salary, but could not retain the new job and was fired within three months. This is a good example of why a person should control expenses and lifestyle instead of looking for a bigger job with a higher salary and failing in it.

Best cities for your RFJ

In India, it is always better to work in a bigger city—Mumbai is the best Indian city to start a career. Why? Because Mumbai teaches you many things, and is safer for women than many other Indian cities. Mumbai teaches you to work hard, work professionally, make new friends and, most importantly, it 'toughens' you. Yes, travelling in Mumbai suburban trains is tough. I travelled by crowded Mumbai trains for the first seven years of my life, but it taught me how to 'survive', how to reach office 'on time' despite all the traffic jams, etc. Our research shows that most of the successful CEOs of India started their career in Mumbai or Delhi in the non-IT industry segment, started in Bengaluru/Chennai if in the IT Industry. So do not get intimidated by big cities.

Working in Mumbai

Mumbai is a land of dreams where many people come with the hope of getting a job to make a living. In Hindi, they call it 'Sapno ki Nagri'. It is also the financial capital of the country having institutions like the Reserve Bank of India (RBI) and the National Stock Exchange (NSE). Many multinational companies and Indian companies have either their head offices or their branches in this city. Industries like banking, finance, IT, arts and entertainment, travel and tourism, etc. flourish in this place, giving way to numerous job openings.

The biggest advantage of working in Mumbai is that it toughens you up as a person. You get used to the multicultural lifestyle of this city. The work style is very professional and westernized due to the large number of MNCs operating from Mumbai.

It is a densely populated city, and many people come into the city to look for a job and make a living. It is generally expensive when compared to other metros and cities in India. So if you are planning to move to this city, you need to prepare well in advance and make a lot of arrangements. Things you might want to consider before you move into this city are listed below.

Working long hours

There are ample job opportunities available for both skilled and unskilled people. But the competition is high. Considering the immense competition, the work timings also differ from other places. You need to work for longer hours and also travel at least 45 minutes one way.

Cost of living

The cost of living in Mumbai is around 30 per cent higher than other cities in the country. Be it rent, travel, food, etc., you need to shell out some extra money for living a comfortable life in this city. Therefore, the salary paid to an employee who is working in Mumbai is generally higher when compared to other cities, but you end up spending that extra salary.

Local travel and safety

Travelling in Mumbai is a pain especially if you choose to use your own vehicle. Distances, heavy traffic jams and bad roads can cause a lot of trouble. So people living there generally opt for local trains. Mumbai is generally considered a safe place to work.

Working in other metros

India is a developing nation and so are its cities. There are five 'tier-1' cities that can be termed as metros or metropolitan cities of the country. They are:

◻ Mumbai
◻ Delhi
◻ Bengaluru
◻ Kolkata, and
◻ Chennai

We have seen factors to consider while working in Mumbai. Now let us look at working conditions in other metros.

Working in Delhi

Delhi is our national capital. It is home to our Parliament and many public sector units (PSUs) are headquartered here. Apart from this, many multinational and Indian companies operate from Gurgaon, which is adjacent to Delhi and is part of the National Capital Region (NCR) which contributes to its development. Sectors like IT/ITeS, media, tourism, banking, telecommunications, etc. provide numerous employment opportunities to people. The cost of living in this city is as high as Mumbai. The local transport system is fairly good as you have the metro rail, buses, taxis, etc. Many young people from outside Delhi cannot afford to live in Delhi, and therefore, stay in Noida in Uttar Pradesh (very close to Delhi). The only thing that troubles this city is the higher level of crime when compared to other cities. The climatic conditions are also extreme—very dry and hot during summer, humid during monsoon, and extremely cold during winter.

Working in Bengaluru

Bengaluru is developing at a fast pace. It is popularly known as India's Silicon Valley. Many MNCs have set up their IT centres here. Especially, huge development of the IT industry has caused a massive real estate boom in the city, so rentals are on the higher side. The health care facilities are good. The cost of living is, however, less when compared to places like Delhi and Mumbai. The best part about Bengaluru is its climate. It is very pleasant all through the year. Two-wheelers/autos are mostly used as the local means of transport. Again, huge traffic jams and distances are a cause of concern.

Working in Kolkata

Kolkata is a city where the people and culture are very supportive. The biggest advantage is that the cost of living is very low. You may have trouble with the Bengali language spoken there and also with the food that you get, especially if you are a South or a North Indian. The local transport system is good with low-cost taxis plying. But the disadvantage of this city is that the professionalism quotient is low when compared to other metros. People working here may follow the 'no stretch' culture.

Working in Chennai

Chennai is the fastest growing city in the fields of Information technology and manufacturing. If you belong to these verticals, then the growth factor will certainly be high. Many companies have their southern regional offices in Chennai. When it comes to challenges, then food, language and the weather are some of the biggest. Many restaurants are available, but if you want North Indian food, it is expensive. So keeping in mind that you are moving as a fresher with stipulated budget, dining in costly places on a daily basis may not be possible. The weather conditions are not so pleasant, and language is also a concern as most of the locals prefer to converse in Tamil.

Looking for a job overseas

All the factors regarding looking for a job outside your hometown hold good for this section as well, but with a little more importance because you will need extra income to live a comfortable life overseas. Apart from that, the most important and vital factor is getting a 'visa' to work in that particular country. The situation is a little trickier if you haven't applied for a job and are planning to travel without a job. But if you have attended an interview, then, normally, your employer has to get you a work visa. There is a lot of research that you need to do before you look for a job overseas.

Deciding which country you want to work in

Your first step will be doing a research and zeroing on a country that you want to work in. You need to find out about the economic conditions of that country, the weather, the people and many more aspects before applying for a job. Generally, the working conditions differ from region to region. For example, if you find a job in the Middle East (e.g. Dubai or Muscat), then you must be ready to work long hours initially, because people there believe in spending at least ten hours at work.

Once you decide on which country you want to go, you need to visit the respective embassy website to find out more details and what exactly you need to do to relocate there.

Apply for a visa

Once you collect all the details, if you have a passport, then you need to apply for the work visa. Your employer will furnish you with all the documents for visa application. If you do not have a job, then you need to apply for a tourist/visit visa to look for a job, and once you get a job, convert your status to a 'work visa'.

Use networks to look for jobs

Once you have zeroed in on the country, you should start visiting job boards popular in that country and also connect with people living in those countries.

Learn the local language

English is spoken in most countries, but in a few places, it is extremely important to know the local language. For example, if you are moving to Berlin, then you must learn the German language as it will help you communicate easily with the locals there, and if you move to France, then you must learn French. It is always an added advantage if you know the local language as some companies specifically ask for fluency in local languages.

Brush up your skills and acquire required certification

You must make it a point to keep your skills up to date when you work overseas, because you will be competing with people from all over the globe. You need to be very good at what you do. Do considerable research on what skills are required to excel and take the required training. If you are looking for a skill-based role like SAP, Oracle, etc., then you must get the necessary global certification so that it will help you find a role easily.

Saving money

Every job seeker who gets a job in the Middle East is told that he/she will save a lot of money because the income tax rate is low and the employer will provide car, accommodation, etc. This is only a myth. The overseas employer includes all the allowances/benefits in the cost to company (CTC) salary, and so, it is better to work out the savings potential. It is also true that this savings potential will not be achieved in the first four years because you will end up buying a lot of consumer durables like a car, TV, etc., and will also buy a lot of gifts for your family back home. Within four to six years, you may get married and if your spouse wants to move with you, the cost of living will go up. Also, as a bachelor, you may share the room rent with other bachelors, but if your spouse joins you, you will have to rent private accommodation. So, practically, you will start saving only after six years or so.

International exposure

The biggest advantage of working overseas is that you get the experience of working with professionals from many other countries. You become smarter and your communication improves.

Coming back to India

It is important to note that it is not easy to come back to work in India if you start your career in the Middle East. Indian companies do not value the Middle East experience, especially in the initial stages of your career. But the same is not true of the IT industry, where overseas experience in Europe/USA is a big advantage.

7

VARIOUS WAYS TO GET
THE RIGHT FIRST JOB

Why and When do companies recruit from campuses?

Why do companies recruit from campuses? The answer is simple. You get fresh talent in large numbers, at an affordable salary and at a low hiring cost.

Let's take this one by one. Talent means that the candidates are enthusiastic, energetic and are very keen to succeed in life. They have no preconceived notions about work and the employer, and hence, can be moulded to the job role and organization.

Let's take the example of IT companies. Many non-computer science engineers are hired and trained by them because it is easier to train a fresher than an experienced person, who has to 'unlearn' his/her previous work habits and processes before they learn the new company's work habits/processes.

India has over 18,000 BA/BSc/BCom colleges and approximately 3,600 engineering colleges, and over 2.5 million graduates pass out every year. Over 10 million men and women study in these campuses. And all of these campuses conduct their exams in March/April and announce the results in April/May. Nowhere in the world, except for China, can an employer find so many educated young people lining up for jobs.

Campus students are available at a very competitive salary because they are not well trained for the job. If a company is smart, they can hire exceptionally smart graduates by going to the 'right' campus and get candidates at less than the market price. Lastly, the recruitment cost is very low because the companies hire in bulk and the colleges (except IIMs and IITs) do not charge any fees from the employers. So campus hiring makes a lot of sense—if the hiring numbers are large and the employer has large training plans/budgets.

When do the employers hire from campuses?

Even though the students will join in May/June/July of every year, the hiring (offers) will be done much before. MBA colleges have their placement season in September onwards in the second year. Engineering colleges have their placement season starting from the seventh semester. Other graduate colleges (BA/BSC/BCom) have their placement season for January in the sixth semester. Though the above is a guideline, there are likely to be exceptions.

What are campus recruitments?

Recruiting fresh talent from college campuses, be they graduate campuses, MBA campuses, engineering campuses, etc., is called campus recruitment.

This concept came to light in the 1980s when companies went to engineering colleges to recruit engineering trainees and management trainees from only premier institutes/colleges of the country. The main reason was to catch the best talent at their source. Some companies (example, IT/ITeS) hire candidates in bulk, keeping in mind the size of the project/company. They need candidates who can work for longer hours with enthusiasm and zeal. So the best way to hire in bulk is through campus recruitments, as students come with fresh minds and the curiosity to learn and always want to prove their talent.

Therefore, for entry-level positions, companies, with the consent of the college management, conduct campus recruitments where talented students who are in their final year of graduation/ MBA are shortlisted and assessed in the campus itself.

It is a big advantage from your perspective, because as a fresh college graduate, you will not have to bother about applying for various companies and hunt for jobs.

Process of campus recruitment

Companies select and shortlist campuses that have a fairly good name in the city they are present in, because the quality of talented youth in these places is high. Once a campus is selected, they approach the management to take their consent. They then speak to students and explain to them the advantages of working with their company (through pre-placement talks), and also share with them how much they can save over a period of time

Aptitude tests/written examinations/group discussions are conducted for interested candidates. Based on how you perform in these tests, you will be called for a technical interview by a subject matter expert. If you fare well in the technical interview, you will be called for the final interview by the HR team where they will throw some light on your salary and work timings, and gauge your seriousness. After the final interviews are done, a final list of selected candidates is sent to the college and the same is communicated to the students.

Steps in campus recruitment: Diagram explaining the Process of Campus Recruitment

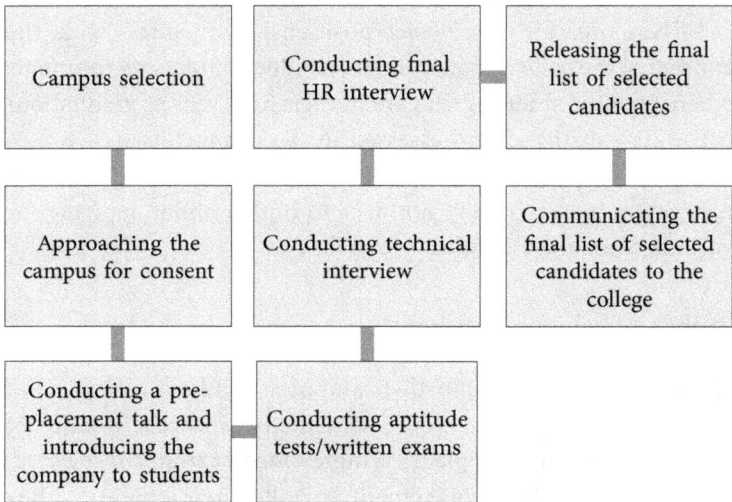

Campus selection	Conducting final HR interview	Releasing the final list of selected candidates
Approaching the campus for consent	Conducting technical interview	Communicating the final list of selected candidates to the college
Conducting a pre-placement talk and introducing the company to students	Conducting aptitude tests/written exams	

What are the advantages of campus recruitments to a job seeker?

Recruiting through campuses is beneficial to companies as it helps them reduce the cost of employment. But they are equally beneficial to students also. Let us look at these in the table below.

Advantages of campus recruitments to a job seeker
Good companies come to your campus. Attending the assessment test, etc. becomes very easy.
You can apply for more than one company at a time. You have a choice of job roles and employers.
Companies will have to share a lot of information when they come to the campus to hire. You can ask them for more information. Thus, you can make an informed choice.

Advantages of campus recruitments to a job seeker
You have a job offer from a good company, whereas your friends are still looking out for jobs.
You have the benefit of being trained by the company as a campus recruitment, as the expectations from you are not very high because companies also realize the fact that you are fresh out of college.
You can join the employer in a group. This helps in settling down in the city of employment and in the company. For example, you can have an apartment and share the cost along with other campus-selected students.
Since large employers come to campus and hence make many offers, your chances of getting an offer are much higher.
You start earning at a very early stage and therefore get to save more money or contribute to family expenses, or start paying back the education loan. College alumni working in the company can be contacted to get more information about the job. The placement office in the college will have data on alumni.
The college placement office can also help in coordinating the interview date, etc.
The interview dates are planned by the placement office so that you can attend multiple interviews without missing any.
The college placement office follows up on the offers, after campus assessments. They ensure that the results are announced quickly.

How to get a job with the help of a reference?

When you are actually looking out for a job, it is always good to inform people and seek their help. It is always beneficial to be an active part of a network or group which can refer you to others for a job. Relatives, friends, classmates, seniors from your college, and friends from social media like Facebook/LinkedIn can refer your CV to their current employer, to a HR head they know, or to a CEO they know.

How does the referee (the person who refers your CV) benefit? Many companies run 'referral programs' and are willing to pay a referral fee if they refer you and you get a job. Many companies also like their employees to work in 'friendly' groups, and hence, ask employees to refer their friends. So, by referring your CV, your friend can get a good name and even earn money in his/her company.

How can your seniors from college help you?

Your seniors in college can also help you in landing your first job. They know the pain of job hunting as they have been through it earlier. If they are doing well, then the HR department respects their views on the next batch of students. The only thing you must do is constantly stay in touch with them and keep up good relations.

They can give you information about job openings and also the work culture in their companies. In a few cases, they could be the ones hiring for a position, and you can get your foot in the door and even get tips on interviews. They can also keep you informed on what is happening in the job market and give you career guidance.

How to get a job with the help of a recruitment consultant?

Who are recruitment consultants? Almost all companies have an in-house HR department which is responsible for hiring candidates for the company. But sometimes, due to huge requirements and time constraints, companies outsource their recruitment process to recruitment consultants. There are many recruitment consultancy firms operating in India, which perform all or parts of the recruiting procedures on behalf of the company.

Every company has specific criteria while hiring candidates for vacant positions. These recruitment firms shortlist the candidates in the initial stage for their clients. Being a fresher, you must look out for a firm that specializes in recruiting freshers. Also, if you are looking at a particular industry, for example—IT, you can look for a consultancy that specializes in hiring for IT. You can search for one in your city and sign up with them. They would help you find a suitable job based upon your qualification, skill-set and preferences.

Why should recruitment consultants help you?

Most consultants get paid for hiring candidates like you. So they are not doing you a favour but are earning money by placing you.

Why are recruitment consultants not keen to meet you?

The number of recruitment consultants getting employment for freshers is very limited. Many specialize in experienced candidates. In such a case, they do not have any fresher requirements and, hence, are not keen to meet you.

How can the fresher recruitment consultants help you?

The fresher recruitment consultants hire: (i) from campuses for big employers; (ii) select freshers from their database and assess them for large corporates, after the campus season is over (see example at www.tmie2eacademy.com); and (iii) select freshers for small and medium enterprises (see example at www.jobsdialog. com). So if your CV is in their database, your chance of getting an interview call letter increases.

How can you reach out to recruitment consultants?

Google and find out the fresher recruitment consultants. Go to their website, register and fill up the form. Find out the person who handles fresher recruitments in that organization and contact him/her over phone/email. Write a powerful covering letter highlighting your strengths and your positive attitude.

If you are unemployed, ask the recruitment consultant to give you a chance to work as an apprentice or freelancer till you get the right first job (RFJ). This way the consultant comes to know you better and will actively help you find the RFJ.

Even if the recruitment consultant does not have any requirement, find out the vacancies from the job board and ask the consultant to refer you to the HR head of the recruiting company. The chances are high that the recruitment consultant will know the HR head.

How to use the Internet to your advantage while searching for a job

The current era is the era of the Internet. Nowadays, job searching has gone online. Just like in the West, many job portals are available in India today which can help you with job search. The next chapter discusses more about online job boards.

Apart from such job boards, the Internet also helps you by providing access to various company websites where you can do research on the job openings available, the board of directors, the company profile, etc. When you are looking for a job, you need information on the following areas.

What jobs can you apply for?

The Internet has a lot of websites to guide you on your personality (example www.queendom.com), and the results of these tests can provide you with a fairly good idea about the type of career that would suit your personality.

Job descriptions online

The Internet can give you detailed job information. Many websites are available. However, most of these websites are meant for US job seekers. A few websites pertinent to the Indian context exist (for instance, www.bestofjobs.in) but the information is scattered. The book, *An Expert's Guide to 100 Entry Level Jobs,* addresses the top hundred entry-level jobs in demand in India. It is written by me and will be published soon.

Who is hiring for the job that you are interested in?

Google search, job board search and company website search can help you identify vacancies.

Preparing for the interview

Many websites help you prepare better. For example, you can get the list of questions that the interviewer can ask from a few websites. You can research about the employer through financial websites such as www.indiainfoline.com.

Connect with people who can help you find a job or give you a reference. By using social networking sites like www.linkedin.com and www.facebook.com, you can easily connect with your seniors from college. So the Internet can help you at every step of your job search. The Internet, thus, has the answers to various questions that may be in your mind.

How to search for a job in newspapers?

One of the ways companies communicate their vacancies is through newspapers, and hence, you need to understand how to use this medium well. Employers advertise in newspapers because they want to reach a larger audience. For example, a newspaper like *The Times of India* is read by over seven million people. A Malayalam paper like *Malayala Manorama* is read by nine million people.

Secondly, as per the Government of India guidelines, government and public sector companies (PSUs) have to compulsorily advertise so that the news of vacancies reaches as many people as possible.

What are the various types of recruitment advertisements?

Most of the recruitment advertisements are in newspapers, both English and vernacular. Newspapers carry two types of advertisements: Appointment Ads which appear once or twice a week in a separate job supplement, and are large ads carrying some information about the company and the job. The second type called 'Classified Ads' appear twice or thrice a week in the 'Situations Vacant' section where companies announce their vacancies. These are small two- or three-line ads.

Sometimes, employers also use radio and TV (TV scrolls are popular) to announce vacancies.

What are walk-in ads?

Walk-in ads are a special type of recruitment ad. Instead of sending your résumé by email, you are required to 'walk-in' to the interview venue, along with a copy of your CV. Here, the walk-in date is very important and normally the walk-in ad appears three to four days before the walk-in interview. The best thing about walk-in ads is that the company will interview and assess all the walk-in candidates and normally announce the result the same day or the next morning. The second advantage is that many people miss an advertisement, but if you 'walk-in', your chances of getting a job are better.

What is Employment News?

This is a special newspaper which carries all government and PSU jobs. So if you are looking for a government/PSU job, you must read this paper which is published once every week in Hindi, English and Urdu. This also has an online edition http://www.employmentnews.gov.in/.

How do I read all the newspapers without buying a copy?

There are two ways. Most papers have an online edition which will carry the recruitment ads (example: www.the hindu.com/classifieds/jobs). The second option is to visit a library near your house and read the newspapers there, noting down the details of the vacancies that you are interested in.

Can I get a job by getting in touch with employers?

With the advent of the Internet, many company websites are accessible from anywhere in the world. Companies also have a specific section where they upload current openings on their websites. They generally call it the 'Careers' section. So you have the comfort of sitting at home and directly applying for jobs by filling in the required details and uploading your résumé in the required format. Once you register with them, your details and your résumé sit it the company's database.

Sometimes, it so happens that the position you have applied for gets filled. But the company contacts you in case there are future job openings that match your profile, and if you are interested, you can take it forward from there.

What can you do if the employers fail to respond?

First, do not apply only to big companies. Too many people

apply and your chances are limited. Apply to smaller and mid-size companies where your chances are better. Do not restrict your applications only to IT companies and MNCs because these companies prefer to recruit only from a select list of colleges. Instead, apply to other industries and sectors like hospitality, banking and financial services, consumer product companies, pharma companies, etc. You will get a better response from these companies.

If you know someone who knows the CEO/HR head, then ask them to forward your résumé to the CEO/HR head after you register online on the company website. This increases your chances.

Lastly, connect with the HR head through social media like Facebook or LinkedIn, share some interesting ideas with the HR head, and send your résumé only after you establish a rapport.

8

JOB BOARDS—A SMART NEW WAY TO GET A JOB

What is a job board?

A job board is a place where employment opportunities are listed by employers. The job board covers jobs across various sectors and employers. The employers can post job vacancies and job descriptions along with other details like company information, salary, years of experience required, desired skills and educational qualifications. This is called a 'job' database.

Similarly any job seeker can register free of cost and post his/her profile on the job boards by filling up a detailed form. This database, called résumé database, is searched by employers who then prepare a shortlist based on their criteria. Thus, job boards have two databases—the job database and the résumé database.

The job seeker can search the job database and apply directly to the employer. An employer can search the résumé database, shortlist candidates and connect with them directly. In simple words, a job board is where an employer and job seeker can connect with each other.

There are numerous job boards available today like naukri.com, monsterindia.com, timesjobs.com, freshersworld.com, etc. These job boards charge the companies who want to place their job vacancies on the job site, but do not take any money from the candidate who wants to search for job openings. Companies also opt for this method of advertising jobs as it is economical compared to newspaper ads.

Any candidate who is familiar with computers and can operate the Internet can visit these job boards. In most of the sites, navigation is user-friendly. They provide various tips to candidates looking for a job, and also allow them to upload their résumés online so that employers can take a look and shortlist candidates based on their required criteria. Even recruitment consultancy firms take the help of job boards to source the résumés of required candidates.

Job boards thus act as a bridge between a potential candidate and a prospective employer.

List of 10 best job sites/boards that are available to freshers

Name of job site	Brief description
www.naukri.com	Naukri is one of the best job sites available for people who are looking for jobs. It was started in the year 1997. Since then, it has been a front-runner. They serve corporate customers and candidates across all sectors. They also help candidates in résumé building.
www.monsterindia.com	A flagship of Monster Worldwide.Inc. founded in 1994, it has a presence in fifty countries. This site helps candidates explore various opportunities, and helps employers to find a right fit for the job.
www.timesjobs.com	Operates in India and the Middle East. It is owned by the Times Group. It was launched in the year 2004. They focus more on IT industry and retail, BPO, government and advertising jobs.

www.shine.com	This site is owned by HT Media Ltd, one of the most prominent names in the media industry. It was set up with a motive to help candidates find a job according to their skill, location and experience.
www.jobstreet.co.in	Since 1995, jobstreet.com has grown to become one of the leading Internet recruitment websites in the Asia-Pacific region, revolutionizing the way recruitment is done today. This site helps candidates find a job and employers advertise vacancies.
www.careerbuilder.co.in	One of the best job sites for freshers, where there is a wide variety to choose from.
www.careerjet.com	Careerjet is one of the popular job search engines that has been designed in a very user-friendly manner. It lists job openings available on the Internet in one extensive database, by referencing those that originate from recruitment agency websites, company websites and large specialist recruitment sites.
www.naukrihub.com	It is one of the best sites to find jobs and also details about salaries in India. This site is visited by the best headhunters available in the market.
www.freshersworld.com	One of the best job sites available for freshers. They have a database of over 33 lakh fresher résumés with 90,000 résumés being added every month. They are ranked among the top 300 websites in India.
www.placementindia.com	This is one of the best job sites available to job seekers. It lists jobs available in India, USA, UK and the Gulf.

Basic features of a job board

There are certain basic features that every job board has. The success and popularity of job boards depend on the factors mentioned below. The top twelve features of any successful job board are given below.

Job postings: This feature allows the employer to post vacancies.

Post résumé: This feature allows you to post your résumé and fill up a detailed form.

Search jobs: This feature allows you to access the jobs database and select jobs you want to apply for. You can search jobs by company, job role, job location, job description, etc. Once you select the job, you can immediately apply to that employer.

Search résumés: Employers who pay are given a log-in password to search résumés in the résumé database and connect with those people they shortlist.

Broadcast your résumé to recruiters: By paying a fee, you can instruct the job board to send your résumé to the top recruiting consultants.

Résumé writing services: Experts with experience can rewrite your résumé for a fee.

Job alert: You may not be able to visit the job board every day, so this feature notes down your job preferences and informs you, by email, if any new jobs are posted matching your preferences. This is a powerful feature and becomes your 'eyes and ears' on the job board.

Résumé validation: Some job boards offer to validate your résumé by verifying the details presented in it, for a fee. A set of experienced people can talk to you and verify your credentials and record the same in your résumé in the job board. This improves your chances of being shortlisted.

Visual résumé: You can upload your video profile along with a text résumé. This help employers in shortlisting based on your visual appeal.

Articles on tips and careers: Many job boards publish articles by leading experts on tips on résumé writing, interview preparation, etc.

Employer information: Many employers provide detailed information on job boards to brand themselves as the best employers. This tells you that this company will be hiring regularly.

Salary information: Job boards also provide salary information so that you can check what salaries you can expect, or check whether you are getting a fair salary after you get an offer.

How to search for a job on job boards?

When you visit a job board, first select if you are looking for domestic jobs or international jobs. You will find various industries like IT/ITeS, finance, banking, marketing, etc. Based on your interest, you can select a particular industry.

Within the industry specific page, you will find tabs like:

- job role/designation
- location
- expected salary range
- years of experience

Fill in the required details as per your preference and hit the search button. A list of relevant jobs will be displayed.

Job boards also have a list of companies that are hiring currently. You can shortlist companies that you wish to apply for and view the existing job openings available in that company. If you find a suitable role, you can follow the application process as mentioned in the site.

If you wish to specifically look for jobs available in a particular city/location, you can select that option and look for jobs that are available in that particular city. Many job boards also provide mobile applications, where you can download the mobile App onto your mobile and access the site, as and when required, through your phone itself.

Tips for successful job hunting on a job board

The biggest problem in a job board is that you are one among millions of freshers looking for a job. For example, when an employer logs in and searches résumés, the résumés are shown in batches of twenty-five on every page. So if your résumé is the 900th résumé, it will be on the 36th page. Employers may shortlist other résumés before reaching your résumé. To avoid this, you should take the following steps.

Update your résumé regularly: Many employers shortlist only those résumés which are updated recently.

Complete the résumé: Take time and complete the registration form in full.

Use features like video CV: Prepare and make a powerful video of yourself. Since there are not many video résumés, you may stand out.

Use job alert: To get information on jobs as soon as a vacancy is posted. Apply quickly because early response is a big plus.

Regularly visit the job board: Do this to find out the list of big recruiters. Apply to them, one by one. Many online forms have a text box to give three reasons why the employer should hire you, based upon the requirements mentioned in the job posting.

Lastly, only one in thousand freshers may get a job through a job board. So post in as many job boards as possible, keep trying and do not get disappointed easily. The only way to beat the odds is to persevere and keep trying.

9

THE RÉSUMÉ

What is a résumé?

The first thing you need as you start your job search is a résumé. Unless you are an actor or planning to become an entrepreneur, you will need one. The word 'résumé' means 'summary' in the French language. So basically, a résumé is a summary of your education and work experience. This means that it is a summary of your qualifications, skills, training and certification, extra-curricular activities, strengths, and your contact details. It is also called a CV, i.e. *curriculum vitae*.

Did you know Leonardo Da Vinci was the first person to write a professional résumé in 1482? (mashable.com) So résumés have been around for 500 years. By the early twentieth century, résumés were informally written and just a formality that job seekers would write on paper available at the time and hand it over to the employers during meeting. It wasn't till the 1950s that résumés were expected and required by companies. With the advent of computers in the 1970s, résumés became professional.

Your résumé is your first step towards introducing yourself to recruiters/companies looking to hire. You will be surprised to know that a recruiter takes only a few seconds to go through a résumé, sometimes not more than ten seconds. You will literally be making an impression in a few seconds without being physically present. Your résumé will do the talking for you, so write it in a way that the recruiter takes in exactly what you are trying to portray. Don't leave room for any misunderstanding or miscommunication that will hurt your chances. A résumé should also give an indication of what direction you want your career to head. A résumé can get shortlisted for initial assessment. It does not get you a job.

For an interesting infographic on the 500-year history of the résumé, please visit http://theundercoverrecruiter.com/history-resume-info/

Who reads your résumé?

The résumé may be about you, but it is written for someone else. The résumé is important for you, the applicant, because you are sending it across to the recruitment agency or the company looking to hire individuals. The résumé is also very important for the recruiter. This is the only way he can be made aware of your interest in the job opening in the company and your qualifications. This will help him decide whether or not the company should take out time and interview you for the position.

Many times, a recruitment agency will go through résumés and shortlist them for the human resources (HR) department in the company, which will in turn shortlist applicants again. If you fail to make an impression at the first stage, your résumé will not even reach the company. Essentially, your résumé needs to be impressive enough for it to impress all the people involved in the chain till the interview process. You need to differentiate yourself from thousands of other applicants applying for the same position. So it is important to note that though the résumé is about you, it is not written for you. It is written for a person who is going to evaluate you—that means that you should try and understand the reader first, before writing a résumé. For example, an HR person is impressed if you describe your personality well and relate it to the job you are applying for. A technical inductor looks for your technical qualification, your project details, etc. That's why a résumé has many sections to appeal to a variety of evaluators.

What is an employer looking for in your résumé?

A survey was conducted among recruiters to find out what are the most important things they look for in a résumé. The results are given in the chart below.

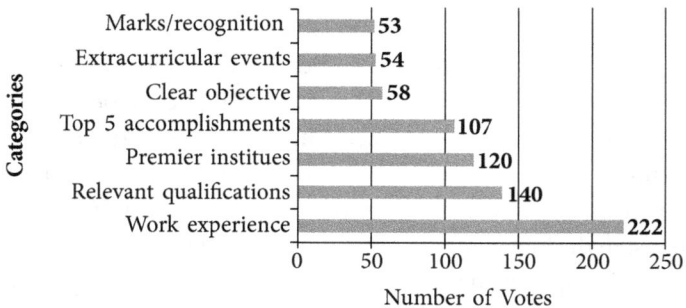

Out of the seven important things mentioned by them, work experience is not applicable to freshers. The remaining six are important.

Relevant qualifications

Clearly, 'relevant' qualification is the most important. Relevant here means relevant to the job that you are applying for. If you are applying for a software job, software qualifications and certification are important. If you apply for a shop-floor job, then engineering/technical qualifications matter. Please note that 'over qualification', i.e. a PhD applying for an engineer job, may also be considered an 'irrelevant' qualification. So please study the job specifications before applying.

Premier institutes

Premier institutes means that if you have studied in a top-ranked school or college, then it should be highlighted. The Indian Institute of Technology (IIT) or the National Institute of Technology (NIT) are considered premier institutes for engineering qualification. The Indian Institute of Management (IIM) and the top ten management institutes in India will be considered premier institutes for management qualification. Similarly, if you studied BCom and your college is ranked at the national or state level, then please mention it.

Top five accomplishments

For a fresher, accomplishments could include ranks in exams, prizes won in competitions, voluntary work with NGOs, sports achievements, etc. Rank the top five accomplishments in the right order—top achievement as Number 1 achievement, and so on. Extra-curricular activities and marks/recognition can be included with the top five accomplishments.

Why your résumé should be unique?

Never copy your friend's résumé by just changing the contact details. There are 2.5 million graduates passing out every year and, according to NASSCOM, only 10-25 per cent graduates are readily employable. This makes it harder for a fresher to find a job. You need to put things in your résumé which set you apart from the other job seekers.

A résumé is your ambassador and it tells what's unique about you. Are you identical to your friend? If no, why should your résumé be identical? Impress them on paper first to impress them in person. Think of yourself as a brand, the employer as the customer, and you have to sell yourself. This is why you should not copy your friend's résumé and just change the contact details and few other sections. An employer receiving thousands of applications does not have the time to go through all the résumés thoroughly. He will quickly glance over it in 10–15 seconds, and if your résumé looks like a hundred others, he will just throw it away. Also, be careful about everything you put inside your résumé as your interview will be based upon that. Customize your résumé to each job and company you apply to, looking at the requirements by the company. Be original, be different and make it interesting.

There are ways in which you can keep your résumé formal and, at the same time, personalize it to stand out. If you are in a creative field like design or advertising, you can come up with innovative ways to represent yourself on paper rather than the typical black and white format of a résumé. You can add colour, branding techniques to make your résumé stand out. With the Internet, a few creative people have started using it to their advantage and people are posting video résumés on YouTube.

A few industries like the retail industry (apparel and luxury goods) have started demanding photographs of the job applicants with the résumé. They require you to interact with customers daily and expect their employees to project themselves in a certain way which reflects its brand image. In the luxury goods market, candidates are expected to be well dressed, well groomed and well spoken to cater to high-end consumers. So make sure that you have a professional photograph taken by a professional photographer.

Sections of a fresher résumé

Your résumé should be comprehensive but also concise, because its fate is decided in just ten seconds.

How long should a fresher's résumé be?

Most of us have been told that we need to limit our résumé to just one page to make it easy for recruiters to go through it. That is not the case according to quickly Indian recruiters. Your résumé can stretch to two pages, provided every bit of information that you cite is relevant and useful.

Contact details

On the résumé, you need to mention your name and contact details. Make sure to mention your current address, mobile number and active email id. All further communication will be made via mobile and email; companies are also sending their offer letters via email now. So ensure that you provide only the active email address.

Career objectives

In this section, you should mention the position you are applying for in the company. It is a good idea to add where you see yourself in the next five to ten years which shows your commitment to stay. So this section needs to be modified whenever you change the role or the company that you are applying for.

Work experience

Being a fresher, you do not have relevant work experience. So you can talk about your internship during college. Don't just mention the time duration and the company where you worked. You should describe it a little bit and discuss how your input was appreciated by the company.

Training and certification

You can discuss any training program you might have undertaken during college. Many students take certificate programs during summer vacations; you can mention that here as well. It does not necessarily have to be related to your education. You could also mention if you have learnt a new language or taken training in graphic design. Please explain why you took that certification, and how it is relevant to the position that you are applying for.

Qualifications

This is where you will mention your academic qualifications. Start by detailing your latest academic degree/diploma and work backwards to the year you finished Class XII. In the Indian context, marks and percentages are important and you can mention those in this section. It helps if you have been a consistent performer, or if you have worked hard and improved your grades as you progressed. If your grades and percentages are poor, do not mention them in the résumé. Highlight if you studied in a premier educational institute either in school or at college. Highlight if you studied in an English medium school.

Extra-curricular activities

Now that all your academic and internship details are filled, you can talk about your hobbies. Mention things you like to do in your free time. It would be good to mention if you are interested in sports, as being a sportsman teaches a lot of good qualities like leadership, teamwork, how to face challenges and how not to be a sour loser—all of these can be mentioned as your strengths. Also mention if you are creative and love art and music. It would be appropriate to mention if you play an instrument or paint in your spare time. But only mention your current hobbies.

Top five accomplishments

As mentioned above, list your top five accomplishments till date. If you have less than five, it is okay but make sure that these accomplishments are significant.

Strengths

You can mention what you think are your strengths. In case you mention that you go to the gym and use weights, do so only to highlight, in so many words, that you care about fitness. Mention your mental abilities—such as your power of concentration, out-of-the-box thinking, etc. Explain how it is relevant to the job that you are applying for. Do not copy your friend's strengths. Identify your strengths and mention them here.

References

You can give names and contact details of your professors and your project leader during internship in this section. Do not give your father's and uncle's names as reference. This needs to be very professional. If you do not have references, it is alright.

How honest should you be in a résumé?

Be very careful about what you put in your résumé. You will need to edit it many times before sending it out to companies. The interviewer will catch on to what you write in your résumé, and question you if anything seems too interesting or false, to test your knowledge and honesty. You never know what the interviewer might ask you. So it's better to be prepared. Companies are very particular about what candidates put in their résumé.

If some information is found to be false after you have been hired, they can and will terminate your employment contract. Very recently, Scott Thompson, the Chief Executive of Yahoo, came under fire for allegedly lying on his résumé. He claimed to have studied computer science for his bachelor's degree from a university which did not start the course until after he had graduated. He had work experience in the field and was, in fact, poached from eBay and brought into Yahoo, but that has not stopped the board of the company from demanding that he be removed for embellishing his résumé.

So the question of lying in your résumé should not arise. Never lie. But the next question is: Should I tell the whole truth?

The answer is not required. You need to share true details only if it will help you. For example, if you got 50 per cent in your Class XII examinations, mentioning this may not help you. So do not mention it. But if you got 95 per cent, please mention it.

In a nutshell, in a résumé, 'tell the truth and nothing but the truth', but be selective in sharing the 'whole truth'.

Online résumé vs. online application form

Job search has gone online and with it the résumés have also gone online. All job websites will ask you to upload your résumé as well as companies require you to send soft copies of résumés via email. Many companies, especially in the IT industry, have their own forms for you to fill on their websites. The information is similar to your résumé. You will need to fill out your contact details, information regarding school and college, your extra-curricular activities, etc.

In the online world, there are two ways in which employers seek information from prospective candidates like you—first, through the online form that you fill, and second, the soft copy/e-copy of your résumé which you will be required to attach to the form. Let's understand the online form first.

Online form

Today, the online form is a very common way to advertise job vacancies for freshers. Why? Because thousands apply for a single vacancy. It is impossible to manually shortlist all applicants in a scientific manner.

Employers ask you to fill up your details in a structured way, so that they can compare with the key criteria and decide to shortlist or reject. The online form also helps in ranking candidates if there are too many applications.

Many employers have a standardized format for all jobs. Some of the employers have started customizing the form for different jobs. The reason for customization is simple: capture information which is important for shortlisting; and the information varies from job role to job role. So the online form is a way of extracting your information in a format of the employer's choice, and hence, you may have to fill up the form, again and again, for every employer.

Soft copy of résumé

On the other hand, the e-copy or soft copy of your résumé is a copy of the résumé in Microsoft Word or PDF format. It is created and stored in a computer, and hence, can be copied and sent any number of times. The advantages of a soft copy of résumé are:

□ it can be formatted and made professionally;
□ you can add colour and fonts to highlight portions of the résumé;
□ you can edit it easily;
□ you can copy it easily; and
□ it can be emailed easily.

The biggest drawback of an e-résumé is that it is difficult for the employer to extract specific information and compare with the criteria—when deciding to shortlist or reject. Software used to extract specific information, called 'parsers', are not very reliable and hence, used only by a few companies.

Why do companies use both the form and the e-résumé?

The answer is simple. Companies use the 'forms' to eliminate and reduce the number of people to interview, and use the résumé during the interview. Only shortlisted résumés are used at the interview stage; the résumé allows an applicant to present his/her personality and helps the interviewer to ask relevant questions of each candidate at the interview.

10

COVER LETTER AND REFERENCE LETTERS

Why do you need a covering letter?

This is a very common question asked by many. But there are very few who actually understand the significance of a covering letter. A covering letter bridges the gap between what is in your standard résumé and what the prospective employer is looking for. It also conveys your seriousness about getting the job. It gives you a chance to make a strong impression about yourself in the employer's mind.

Employers scan thousands of résumés every single day. In the case of fresh graduates, all résumés look alike. Take, for example, a college that has 200 BA graduates passing in 2014, and assume that 50 per cent of them apply for a job in a bank. So 100 résumés will be scrutinized and almost all of them look similar. How do the employers differentiate between which candidate is worth assessing and which one should be ignored? This is where a covering letter pitches in to make a difference. It gives you an opportunity to convey why you are the right fit for the job.

Therefore, the first step is to customize your résumé (as explained in the résumé section of this book). The second step is to write a personalized covering letter which can further differentiate your application from the rest.

What happens if you do not attach a covering letter to your résumé?

If your résumé is strong and you have the right academic credentials, like holding a rank or high percentage of marks, then the role of a covering letter is limited. But if your academic credentials are weak, then a covering letter can definitely help.

Can the covering letter help in interviews?

Yes. If you get shortlisted for interviews, your résumé and covering letter is passed on to the interviewer who may read the covering letter and ask questions based on that. So, a covering letter gives you an opportunity to inform a few key facts about you to the interviewer.

How do you write a good covering letter?

◦ First and foremost, before you write a covering letter, understand the job role. Without this, you will not be able to draft a good covering letter.

◦ Your covering letter has to be short, clear and concise. One of the most common mistakes that people make while writing a covering letter is to repeat the same information that is already mentioned in the résumé. Avoid repeating your résumé.

◦ Study your résumé well. Identify your strengths and weak areas. Elaborate your strengths and condense your weaknesses, and highlight them in your covering letter.

◦ It must contain three to four points explaining why you are a good fit for the position.

◦ Mention your achievement and your specific skills that may be relevant to the job applied.

- Show them that you have done your homework by mentioning something about the company you are applying for.
- Focus and highlight on the area of your expertise.
- If you are writing an email as a covering letter and attaching your résumé, use easy to read and professional fonts. Avoid using calligraphic or italic fonts.
- Always check spellings before sending/submitting your cover letter.
- Mention your email ID and cell number at the bottom.

Convert your negative points into positives in your covering letter

For example, if you are applying for the position of a relationship officer in a bank and your academic performance is low (say 55 per cent), then in the covering letter, you can say, 'Even though my overall marks are only 55 per cent, I would like to highlight that I scored over 75 per cent in subjects like marketing and consumer behaviour, which I liked and which I believe is relevant to the role of a relationship officer.'

Example of Covering Letter for a fresher

Fresh Graduate (first job) cover letter template

Ms Aparna Reddy,
Head HR, TMI Group.

Dear Ms Aparna Reddy,

I am writing to express my keen interest in the role of a recruiter, as advertised by you. As you can see from my CV, I am a graduate with the required qualifications for this role. While I do not possess any relevant experience for this role, I have worked as an apprentice in a similar organization. I would like to highlight the following with reference to my application.

◻ My work ethic is strong and I have gained valuable workplace skills and experience during my period as an apprentice, which would be very valuable for the job advertised. These include listening skills, internal customer orientation, deadline mindset and working in teams.

◻ Your vacancy appeals to me because I prefer to work in a mid-sized organization like yours rather than a very large organization. A mid-sized organization I believe, would help me in building my career.

◻ I have researched the TMI Group on the Internet and have spoken to a few working professionals who have worked with TMI. The impression that I get is that TMI is a professional organization which values youth and energy, and is willing to invest in training of fresh graduates. I would be very happy to work in an organization like yours.

I would be delighted if I were given an opportunity to present my credentials and also share the research that I have done on the TMI Group.

Yours Sincerely,
Your name
Your email ID
Your telephone number

Example of covering letter for an experienced job seeker

Dear Ms Aparna Reddy,

I have read your recent advertisement for the post of a 'recruiter' in your organization with great interest.

I believe my two years of experience gives me the confidence and skills required to excel in the recruiter's job in your organization, because of three reasons that I list below.

- During my two years of experience, I have learnt to connect and network with people, to communicate effectively (both written and oral), and above all, to work within strict deadlines. I am also good at using social media to connect with professionals.
- My past experience also gave me an insight on organizational structure and job roles in any organization, which will be very essential to excel as a recruiter.
- I have the required attitude to succeed as a recruiter as I believe in working hard, following up, being patient, and having a positive mindset at all times.

I request you to give me an opportunity to meet with you to present my credentials and demonstrate my passion for becoming one of the best recruiters in your organization.

Yours Sincerely,
T. Muralidharan
Email:
Phone Number:

Why you need a reference letter and who can give you a good reference letter?

A reference letter is something that will add value to your credibility. When you write a résumé, you claim that you are good at many things. But how truthful are you? If this question pops up in the employer's mind, then it is the reference letter that comes to your rescue.

It is totally different from a character certificate. A reference letter is something that is given when someone is really impressed by your work, your work ethic and your skills, whereas a character certificate confirms your character.

A professional reference can be your superior, your ex-boss, etc. But as a fresher, the best person to give you a reference letter is your teacher, professor and lecturer, or a manager with whom you did a summer project or apprentice work. Imagine you did a project in college. Your professor really liked the way you handled the project. He can state what he liked in your work/ project and also how you were instrumental in making the class learn something new. Then he can give you a reference letter.

Why are reference letters not so popular in India?

Reference letters are very popular in the US, Europe, etc. and are taken very seriously by the employers, because reference letters are issued truthfully and in a balanced way. In India, referrers (those who issue reference letters) try to be helpful and write a lot of positive comments without actually verifying them. So reference letters must be 'truthful' and 'balanced' (i.e. give both positive comments and also areas of improvement).

How to add a reference letter to your résumé?

Ideally, a reference letter should be added at the bottom of your résumé. If you are filling an online form and there is no space in the form, then add the reference letter at the bottom of your covering letter.

Do's and don'ts for getting a reference letter

- Do choose someone who has worked with you.
- Get reference letters from employers, professors, teachers

and anyone else who is familiar with your work ethic (these people are called referrers).

▫ Tell the referrer why you need the reference letter. Do send a thank you note afterwards to the referrer.

▫ Don't put pressure on the referrer to write what you want them to write.

▫ Don't ever forge reference letters.

▫ Don't choose someone only for their title. Pick someone who has a title *and*; knows you well.

▫ Don't choose someone who is a poor writer.

▫ Don't be surprised if the person you are asking for a reference letter asks you to write a draft of the letter which they will later modify and sign. This is common practice.

Sample reference letter

Sub: Reference letter for Mr T. Muralidharan

I have known Mr Muralidharan (TM) for over a year. He worked intensively on a summer project with me from April '13 to June '13 and he has been in touch with me since then. During my work interactions with him, I noticed the following:

▫ He is passionate about his work;

▫ he is an excellent communicator both orally and in writing. His presentations and written reports were well received by my team; and

▫ he sticks to his deadlines. If he needs any revision in deadlines, he takes my permission.

I have given him feedback on the following areas of improvement:

▫ In his position, he sometimes becomes idealistic; he must

be practical also; and

◻ in his enthusiasm for learning, he takes on too many tasks; he should learn to say 'no' sometimes, so that the tasks can be distributed to others.

I believe he will be an asset in any organization which values youthful energy and creates opportunities for freshers to learn and contribute.

I wish him the very best in his career.

Raghunathan
Senior Manager, ABC Logistics Ltd.

11

APTITUDE TESTS

What do aptitude tests assess?

An aptitude test is an exam to determine a person's suitability for a job or a set of activities in a job. It is not a knowledge test. Aptitude tests are typically administered online to filter candidates.

What do aptitude tests measure?

There are many types of aptitude tests: verbal ability; numerical and quantitative ability; reasoning ability; and data interpretation ability.

Verbal ability measures your ability to do the following: spotting errors; completing sentences using the right words; synonyms and antonyms; sentence formation and improvement; change of voice; comprehension; logical ordering of sentences; and verbal analogies (source: www.indiabix.com).

Numerical and quantitative ability measures your ability to do the following: basic arithmetic, including addition, subtraction, division and multiplication; and percentages. Numerical reasoning ability measures your ability to interpret, analyze and draw conclusions. You will be given data in the form of tables or graphs and asked to answer questions. You will have to understand the data given, analyze and interpret the data, and answer the question.

Reasoning ability covers three aspects: verbal reasoning; numeric reasoning; and abstract reasoning. Verbal reasoning is the ability to understand the reason using words. This is more important for managerial jobs. Numerical reasoning is the ability to understand and use numerical concepts, and to clarify the relationship between numbers. Abstract reasoning is the ability to view information outside the range of previous experience.

In a typical verbal reasoning test, you will be given a passage to read and be given a few statements about the passage. You have to decide whether the statement is 'true', 'false', or 'cannot say'. In a typical numerical reasoning test, you will be given data in a table or graph form, and you will have to answer a few questions on the data.

Tips on how to prepare for aptitude tests

Tip 1—Practise, practise and practise
Practice helps to familiarize you with the test pattern and test questions. It helps you to do the test faster.

Tip 2—Stay focused on your weaknesses
Take practice tests and find out which questions you are struggling with. Start from the basics, taking basic-level tests on these topics, and slowly build up your confidence by attempting more and more difficult questions.

Tip 3—Go for coaching classes if you can afford them
You can ask questions to the instructor at coaching classes if you don't understand something, and seek a simple explanation.

Tip 4—Learn shortcuts
For many topics, find short cuts through repeated practice. This will cut down the time you spend while taking the test.

Tip 5—Sleep well before the exam

Do not desperately study till the last minute. Sleep well the night before. Relax your mind.

Tip 6—Study in small groups

Ideally, two or three people studying together helps in motivating you when studying. And you will find learning from your friend much easier than from a book.

Tip 7—Use the Internet to find test sites and study material

There are excellent websites available to take tests like www. practiceaptitudetests.com and www.aptitudetests.com

12

WRITTEN AND TECHNICAL TESTS

What do written tests measure?

A technical test measures the technical ability/capability of candidates. Technical tests are usually conducted for job roles in IT, scientific and engineering sectors. Technical tests not only measure technical aptitude but also logical thinking, quantitative ability, and the reasoning ability of a candidate.

Technical ability/aptitude—Technical ability or aptitude is nothing but a candidate's ability to solve technical issues that arise at the workplace. Technical tests do not mean engineering or IT subjects only. Technical tests can be in any domain including psychology, chemistry, etc. Typically, in a technical test, you will be asked to solve technical problems or give technical solutions, and the questions will be from the subjects in your curriculum.

Logical thinking—This test measures how logical you are in taking decisions at work and how you react to a situation.

Quantitative ability—This test measures how good you are with numbers.

Reasoning ability—This test measures how good you are at solving puzzles, and in your reasoning power.

Verbal ability—This test measures how good you are at reading, identifying errors, your grammar and verbal ability to express your ideas.

The purpose of these tests is to objectively eliminate candidates who have poor knowledge in the subjects they studied. But the focus is on the fundamentals of the subject and not on advanced concepts.

How to prepare for a written technical test?

Since the written technical tests are designed to measure your subject knowledge and the focus is always on the fundamentals of the subject, your preparation too should focus on the fundamentals. Please note that the interviewer knows that you are only a graduate (not a doctorate in the subject), but also knows that if your fundamentals are wrong, then your advanced subject knowledge will also be very weak.

Get your foundation concepts right. For example, if you are attempting a technical test of a software company, then you must have a strong grip on programming languages like Java, C, C++, etc. If you are a commerce graduate applying for an accounting job, then revise accounting principles, basic journal entries, etc.

Revise all formulae as this will help you solve problems. Take sample written technical tests available on the web and keep practising till you score maximum marks. Different companies follow different patterns of written tests. Talk to your seniors who have taken the test in the previous year.

The second aspect is 'smart' preparation. Sometimes, you do not have time to revise all the fundamental courses. In such a case, research on the company—its products and how do they manufacture (this applies only if the employer is a manufacturing company and you are taking an engineering/technology test), and identify technical areas relevant to the company.

For example, if you are a mechanical engineer applying for a production job in a car parts company, read up on the fundamentals of internal combustion, transmission, hydraulics, etc. which are used in every car. On the other hand, if you are applying for an accountant's post, and you find out that the company is using 'TALLY' software, read up on the TALLY software fundamentals.

Top ten tips on how to take a written/technical test

The top ten tips that will prove useful when you are actually taking a written technical test are given below.

1. Don't panic if your mind goes blank; it happened many times in my schooldays and also in my IIT entrance test. Just relax by taking deep breaths; the 'blankness' will go away.

2. Don't panic if the paper appears to be tough. Please note that everyone gets the same paper. If it is tough for you, it is tough for everyone.

3. Check out the number of sections, the time per section, and calculate average time per question. Read the exam instructions at least twice. Find out if there are negative marks for wrong answers. This is important.

4. If you do not understand a question, stop and re-read the question. Read slowly and you will understand better. Do not be in a hurry to answer a question. Read it twice at least. It may be a 'tricky' question.

5. Start from the first question. If you do not know the answer, please move on. You can come back later. Do not get stuck at a question more than the average time calculated in point 3 above.

6. First attempt the easy questions which you are confident (but not overconfident) about. This will boost your confidence.
7. Study the multiple choice answers carefully. Some of the choices may be completely wrong. Eliminate the answer by putting an X against the 'obvious' wrong answer. This reduces your choice of answers. If there are no negative marks, then you can guess from the reduced list.
8. Mark questions which you want to come back to later. When you come back, focus only on the marked questions.
9. Underline 'key words' in the questions. This way, you will not miss out on the 'core' of the question.
10. Don't panic if you are not able to attempt all the questions. Many tests are designed for that. It is better to get a few questions right than many questions wrong.

13

GROUP DISCUSSIONS

Why do companies conduct group discussions?

First, let's understand what a group discussion (GD) is. The GD is a group activity. Eight to twelve people are asked to sit together and discuss a topic given by an assessor. Typically, the discussion lasts for twenty to thirty minutes. The assessor watches the discussion and takes notes. In the end, candidates are given scores and based on these scores, some candidates are eliminated and the rest go on to the next stage. Most GDs are conducted in English, though they are sometimes also conducted in the vernacular.

The primary purpose of a GD is to assess communication skills, communication style, leadership style, etc. Communication skills include how well you listen, how you talk, etc. In communication style, you are assessed on how you interrupt the other party, how you argue, how well you are using logic while arguing, etc.

In leadership style, you are assessed on how well you are able to convince the other members during the GD, and whether you are using data and statistics to prove a point, etc.

The ultimate purpose is to understand whether you can communicate well, in a logical and cogent way, when you join the company and work in a team or communicate with customers.

Typical GD evaluation form

A typical GD evaluation form filled by an assessor is shown below.

Model GD evaluation form

GD Group # :							
Conducted on:							
Assessed By:							
Candidate Score on the topic out of 10 maximum							
S. No.	Topic	Candi-date 1	Candi-date 2	Candi-date 3	Candi-date 4	Candi-date 5	Candi-date 6
1	Clarity of thought						
2	Ability to interact with the group						
3	Commu-nication skills						
4	Leader-ship traits						

The four attributes are elaborated below.

Clarity of thought: Talks with facts, has deep understanding of the topic, brings in relevant and original points, can apply real life learning and academic knowledge.

Ability to interact with the group: Is a contributor, helps other team members with ideas and perspectives, does not interact without valid reason, summarizes and steers the group to a conclusion.

Communication skills: Has a command over the language, ability to put across ideas fluently, is an active listener.

Leadership traits: Holds the group's attention while speaking, assumes the role of leader naturally, forceful and yet persuades and convinces the group, aligns and steers the group to the common agenda.

Types of GD and topics covered

A GD is nothing but debating different ideas, views and perceptions of a group of people on a particular topic. Candidates who clear the written test are called for a GD. There are different types of GDs.

Knowledge-based GD's—These are based on general socioeconomic topics. Here, a candidate is assessed on how well he is able to articulate his thoughts on general topics. For example, child labour, dowry system in our country, tradition of sati etc.

Controversial GDs—These type of GDs are argumentative and emotional in nature. Candidates are given a controversial topic, where some people talk for and some against the topic. For example, 'Telangana turmoil in Andhra Pradesh', or 'Should there be reservation for SC/STs in government jobs?'

Opinion-based GDs—A topic is given to candidates where each of them express their opinion on a particular topic and the group discusses the different opinions. For example, 'Owning credit cards—a curse or a blessing?'

Case-based GDs—These GDs are case-based. A particular case is taken up by the group where all members discuss and find a solution to a problem. For example, 'Ragging in educational institutions.'

Abstract GDs—These are GDs that crop up out of the blue. You are sitting with your friends and while discussing various other things, all of you suddenly start discussing/debating one topic. For example, 'Vegetarians and non-vegetarians are both the same.'

The topic for a GD will be decided by the moderator/assessor depending upon the type of GD. It is a good idea to visit websites like www.careerride.com and www.managementparadise.com to get a list of topics.

Given below are ten sample topics.

1. Business and ethics—do they go together?
2. Are women better managers?
3. Cut in electricity bills—is it really reasonable?
4. Should tuitions be banned?
5. Have computers resulted in unemployment?
6. Good politicians are difficult to find in India
7. Youth in India are becoming greedy by the day
8. Minimum wage—why should we have a minimum wage, or why not?
9. The Nostradamus Code
10. Bribery in business

Tips for excelling in GDs

Believe in yourself: The mantra for success is, 'believe in yourself'. Nothing can stop you from being successful if you have belief and faith in your abilities. You will be able to participate well and share your views and opinions with everyone.

Use your networking skills: Before the GD starts, build a good rapport with people who will be participating with you in the GD, as it will help you get allies during the GD.

Communicate effectively: Communication is the key. If you are able to articulate your thoughts well by talking crisply and to the point, without beating around the bush, you will stand out in the group and attract attention.

Talk more on the subject rather than focusing and stressing on personal achievements: Some people go with a false notion of building an impression by highlighting personal achievements and qualifications. You should always focus on the topic/case/subject and speak.

Concentrate and listen well: You must be an active listener and pay attention to what others are saying, so that you don't repeat the same point that others have already made. If you do repeat things people and the assessor will immediately understand that you are not paying attention to what is being discussed, or that you do not have anything new to contribute.

Be tactful: Sometimes, it may so happen that people will not give you a chance to put forward your views as they want to prove a point. But you should tactfully raise your voice and intervene without being aggressive.

Be calm and composed: Your body language speaks volumes. You must maintain a straight sitting posture by placing your hands over the table and bending a little forward as it looks professional. You must avoid fidgeting with your hair, pen, etc. as it gives an impression that you are not serious.

Note down important points spoken: If you want to reply to any important point that is being discussed, always make a note of the same in your notepad/book.

Keep your emotions at bay: Don't let your emotions hamper your confidence and your speech. If you disagree with anyone on any point, say it in a balanced manner rather than becoming emotional and making silly statements.

Display your leadership skills at the right point: At any point if you feel that the discussion is not leading to any proper conclusion, then intervene and display your leadership skills by reminding the group that they are here to tackle a situation and find an appropriate solution. By doing so, you will send the right signals to the judging panel about your leadership abilities. Further, when interjecting:

- **Use data and statistics to prove your point:** Make sure that the data is correct. State the source of information. Automatically the group starts following you;
- **Don't say I agree with you and then state exactly the opposite view:** People can see through your tactics; and
- **Don't speak too much:** Allow everyone to speak. Invite those who are quiet to speak. This is a good leadership trait.

14

THE INTERVIEW PROCESS

This chapter examines the interview process—the types of interviews, preparing for interviews, questions you should ask, questions the interviewer may ask, etc. Some points may be discussed in more than one section. These are being repeated to emphasize their importance in the interview process.

Different types of interviews

There are various types of interviews. You need to be familiar with all of them and need to understand how to tackle them. They include the following: telephonic interviews, personal interviews, video conferencing/Skype interviews, panel interviews, stress interviews, campus interviews, and technical interviews.

Before moving on to the various types of interviews, it would be pertinent to look at how you should prepare and conduct yourself in general during an interview. Tips on the various types of interviews mentioned above are also discussed in this chapter.

How you should conduct yourself during an interview

How well you fare in the interview depends on how you present yourself. An interview can be stressful for you considering the fact that you have very limited interview experience. Therefore, you must keep in mind some very important points before and while attending an interview.

Research the company beforehand

Before attending an interview, you must always do some research about your prospective employer and the job role for which you are being interviewed. By doing this, you will be able to answer well when interviewers ask you questions like: 'What do you know about our company?' 'What are our products?' 'Who are our competitors?' etc.

Arrive early at the venue

Being punctual is something you should practise in everyday life as it will help you always. You must always arrive fifteen minutes early at the interview venue. It helps you settle down and relax.

Be neatly groomed and dress formally

You must always maintain personal hygiene. Use a mild deodorant or perfume. Ensure that your mouth doesn't smell. Neatly comb your hair. Men must always shave before attending an interview.

The first impression is the best impression. Therefore, you must dress right for an interview. It gives the interviewer an idea of how serious you are about getting the job as well as your dressing sense. Don't wear jazzy or bright coloured clothes. Opt for subtle and earthy colours as they are pleasing to the eye. It is not essential for women to wear 'western' clothes. Women can wear a sari or salwar kameez. (See section 14.3 for further details).

Be confident

When you are called inside the interview room, walk straight, with a slight smile on your face. Greet the interviewer by giving a firm handshake. Look into the eyes of the interviewer and respond to questions asked, as it will make them feel that you are confident about yourself and your answers.

Maintain a composed body posture

Your body posture can speak volumes. It is very important to maintain the right body posture. Sit straight, leaning slightly forward. Do not lean backward or bend too much forward. Do not play with the pen or your hair. Do not come to the interview with a chewing gum in your mouth.

Answer to the point

Don't exaggerate.

Listen carefully

To answer correctly, you must first listen to what is being asked. If you are not clear about the question, ask the interviewer to repeat the question

Say, 'I don't know', if you don't know the answer

If you are asked a tricky question, and you do not know or are not confident about your answer, then say, 'I am sorry, sir, but I do not know the answer to this question.' The interviewers are fine if you don't know the answer, but would not like to listen to any faulty or wrong answers. If you do not know the answer, it is a good idea to tell the interviewer that you can find out the answer. Ask where can you research, who can you ask, etc. to find the answer. This is reassuring to the interviewer.

Conclude the interview on a positive note

Thank the interviewer for his/her time. Ask them any further information that you need to know about the company, like their work culture, on-boarding process, etc.

How to dress for an interview

- You need to dress in formal wear and make sure it is neat and clean. Ironed/pressed shirt or starched saris (if cotton) are recommended.
- Men should wear formal pants with a belt and full sleeve shirts with formal dark conservative leather shoes. Well-polished shoes are a must.
- If you are wearing a jacket and tie, make sure that the colour matches.
- Girls can wear a suit or a sari. Western clothes are not mandatory except for certain MNC interviews.
- Girls should wear little or no jewellery. Same goes for the boys.
- Make sure your hair is combed properly so it doesn't look untidy. Men should get a haircut. Girls can tie their hair back.
- Men should not use oil on their hair.
- You should have well-manicured nails.
- In case you are chewing gum, get rid of it before the interview.
- You should wear deodorant or perfume but it should not be too strong.
- Carry a portfolio or a briefcase.
- Carry a pair of shirts/socks in the rainy season. Your dress can get wet or dirty in the rainy season while reaching the venue.
- Go to the washroom fifteen minutes before the interview, comb your hair and tidy up.
- Women should avoid high heels unless they are very comfortable.

Telephonic interviews

When you're actively searching for a job, it's important to be prepared for a telephonic interview at a moment's notice. You never know when a recruiter or an employer might call and ask if you have a few minutes to talk. That is why it is very important to put down your latest telephone numbers, including your mobile number.

A telephonic interview is where recruiters screen potential candidates after selecting a few based upon their cover letter and résumé. Thus, this type of interview is conducted over the phone mainly for the purpose of initial screening and shortlisting of candidates.

This helps the recruiter narrow down the number of prospective candidates to be assessed in a personal interview. Interview panels don't have time to conduct personal interviews for everyone. So they nominate a junior technical or HR person to conduct the telephonic interview in order to weed out the 'not suitable' candidates. Telephonic interviews are also used to screen outstation candidates to minimize the travel cost of candidates.

You will be informed prior to the interview about the date and time of the interview. You will need to confirm and reconfirm your telephone numbers.

You must be clear in your communication and answer to the point during telephonic interviews.

Tips for a telephonic interview

- Keep your résumé in clear view, on the top of your desk or tape it to the wall near the phone, so it's at your fingertips when you need to answer questions.
- Have a shortlist of your accomplishments available to review.

- Have a pen and paper handy for taking important notes.
- Turn the call waiting option on your phone into off mode so your call isn't interrupted.
- If the time isn't convenient, ask if you could talk at another time and suggest some alternatives.
- Clear the room—turn off the stereo and the TV; close the door.
- Unless you're sure your cell phone service is going to be perfect, consider using a landline phone rather than your cell phone to avoid a dropped call or an interrupted line.
- If the question is not clear, politely ask them to repeat the question. It is also a good idea to repeat the question before you answer. This is done to ensure you have understood it correctly.
- Make your answers short and to the point. Interviewers are normally impatient and will not listen to long speeches.
- Do not interrupt the interviewer, except when you cannot hear or understand. Always interrupt politely. Wait for a break in the interviewer's talk.
- When you finish your answer, ask, 'Does it make sense?' It is a way of getting feedback.
- In the beginning, understand and agree on the duration of the call, so that you can plan better and postpone all other activities.
- If the interviewer continues beyond the agreed time, it is normally a good sign. So tell the interviewer that you are agreeable to extend the time and let him/her know that you are keen to engage.
- If you are unable to extend the time because of prior commitments, then politely suggest another time to continue the interview.

◻ When signing off the phone call, thank the interviewer, tell him/her that you enjoyed the call and that you are keen on continuing the discussions with the employer.

◻ Before signing off, ask what will be the next step? This is a professional way of finding out the interviewer's reaction to your interview. If the interviewer says he will set up a meeting with Mr X in a few days, then you have scored. If the interviewer says, 'I don't know, we will have to think about this,' then your interview hasn't gone off well.

Personal interviews

This type of interview is conducted by calling you to the office. Make sure that you are smartly turned out and look professional, carry a pen and anything else that you might need. You will be asked to tell the interviewer about yourself, your qualifications, your strengths and challenges, etc. You need to answer with confidence to create a strong impression. Non-verbal communications are also assessed during personal interviews; for instance, how you sit (best to sit up straight and not slouch), how much eye contact you make, etc.

Video conferencing/Skype interviews

Since hiring has gone global, interviewing a candidate through video Skype (www.skype.com) or Google Talk has become necessary to expedite the interview process. Hiring managers and recruiters can conduct the first round of interviews more quickly, save on transportation costs, and get the interview process completed much faster.

Video interviews are not very common in India except in

IT/ITeS industry, especially for freshers. But if you happen to be in an industry which requires you to work in another city, or a job opening that you are interested is available in another city, this could be an option for the recruiters.

What is the difference between a telephonic interview and a video interview?

The difference is that in a video interview, interviewer can see you while you answer his/her questions. This can prevent impersonation which can happen in telephonic interviews. More importantly, your body language and other non-verbal communication are also visible to the interviewer.

What is the biggest challenge in video interviews?

It is the Internet bandwidth at the interviewee's end (your end). If the bandwidth is too low, the pictures freeze and the audio is also not good. In such a case, see if you can get a quiet room at a cyber café, or some other venue, where the bandwidth is good and you are comfortable and can be undisturbed. In the case of telephonic interviews, the bandwidth is not a big issue because audio files are not as big as video files.

Tips for video interviews

Plan in advance

- Make sure you send relevant materials like covering letters, résumé, etc. to the recruiter in advance.
- Arrive early so you have time to get seated and settled.
- Learn about and get used to using Skype or Google Talk software. In any case, set up a dummy interview with a friend, one day before the actual interview, to go through

the process and get comfortable with matters such as muting or increasing the volume, etc.

What to wear

▢ Dress professionally like you would while attending a personal interview.

▢ Don't make the mistake one candidate did! He wore a coat, dress shirt and tie, presuming that only the top half would show. However, when he stood up the interviewer saw a full-length view, including the shorts and slippers he was wearing.

During the video interview

▢ Make sure the table is clean and neat. You don't want to distract the interviewer.

▢ Be aware that the microphone picks up all the noise in the room. Don't tap your pen or shuffle papers.

▢ Make eye contact. If you don't, the camera will be focused on the top of your head.

▢ Use the picture-in-picture feature so you can see how you appear.

Other tips: Refer to tips for telephonic interview section for more tips.

Panel interviews

Here, a panel of members will be present to interview you. Each of them will quiz you on various matters and, at the end of the interview, each member of the panel will individually score each candidate. Finally, the panel reaches a consensus to recommend suitable candidates.

Stress interviews

These are conducted to test how you handle stressful situations. Nowadays, there is a lot of stress involved in jobs. Therefore it becomes very important for companies to see how well a candidate can handle stress. So, during stress interviews, you will be asked difficult questions and the interviewer may also be 'rude' to you to provoke you. The panel or the interviewer will assess how well you are able to handle the situation without getting furious, aggressive, nervous or scared.

Campus interviews

As a student, you will initially attend a lot of campus interviews. Many organizations will come to your college, conduct a written exam, and thereafter, a personal interview, following which they may or may not shortlist you for the job, depending upon how well you performed.

Technical interviews

These interviews are conducted to test your technical aptitude. You can read in detail about technical interviews in the next chapter.

A list of questions to expect in an interview

1. Tell me about yourself.
2. What are your qualifications? Why did you choose that qualification?
3. What are your top three strengths and weaknesses?
4. Why do you think this is the right job for you?
5. Where do you stay? How do you plan to commute to work?

6. Will you continue enhancing your qualifications? If yes, how?
7. What do you know about our company?
8. Why do you think you will be a good team player? Can you give some examples?
9. Can you handle pressures? If yes, how do you respond to work pressure?
10. What are your expectations from the company?
11. Where do you see yourself five years from now?
12. What will you do beyond working hard to achieve your goals?
13. What are your hobbies?
14. Are you ready to work in shifts? Can you work late?
15. How important is effective communication according to you?
16. How many hours are you ready to put into work?
17. Are you willing to relocate to another city?
18. What are your expectations in terms of compensation?
19. Will you be ready to work during weekends if necessary?
20. Do you have a valid Indian passport?
21. Given this situation, how would you resolve the issue?
22. How important is this job for you?
23. What motivates you to come to work?
24. Give me two reasons why I should hire you instead of someone who is more qualified than you?
25. Describe your dream job.
26. Have you understood the job? If yes, what are the top three deliverables for this job?

Questions you need to ask the employer

At the end of the interview, the interviewer will give the interviewee (you) a chance to ask questions. This is a great opportunity to ask the right questions which leave the right impression about you.

An ideal candidate is someone who seeks clarifications at the end of the interview. Yes, during interviews, you will definitely be given a chance to ask questions. The questions you ask tell a lot about you, your priorities and your mindset. Here, the interviewer's aim is to check how serious and inquisitive you are about the job and the company.

You can pose questions to the interviewer about the company, job, employees, etc. But make sure you do not ask questions about your salary or leave benefits as they will not appreciate answering these questions during the first interview. Therefore, act sensibly and ask the interviewer intelligent questions that will send out positive signals.

Questions you should ask at the end of the interview

- What would be my top three deliverables if I am chosen for this role?
- What do you think are the top three qualities a person should have to do this role better?
- What do you like the most about your company?
- How can I add more value beyond the role requirements?
- How does one advance or grow in the company?
- What is the organization's work culture?
- Who will carry out my appraisals if I'm recruited?
- What are the future plans of the company?
- When will a decision be made on the successful candidate?
- May I contact you if I have other questions? Can you share your contact details?

Why do interviewers ask questions? What are they trying to assess?

As mentioned earlier, the interviewer will ask many questions and will listen and interpret the answers. But ultimately, he/she has to fill up an interviewee form. So the purpose of asking is to finally interpret against the data to be filled in the interview assessment form. For example, if they are scoring on communication skills, then the score will depend on the ability to understand and answer each question.

□ *What are your strengths and weaknesses?*
Why they ask: They want to know what you bring to the table and how your strengths and weakness are relevant to the job. They also want to know if you are aware of your strengths and weaknesses

□ *Do you prefer to work by yourself or as part of a team?*
Why they ask: They want to know if you can work unsupervised and if you can get along well with the team in the company.

□ *Why did you leave your last job?*
Why they ask: Can the reasons repeat in the job for which you are being interviewed.

□ *What do you think this job involves?*
Why they ask: They want to know if you've done your research.

□ *How did your last job prepare you for this job?*
Why they ask: They want to know what your skill-sets are and how you apply your knowledge. They also want to know how much training you'll need.

What you should never do in an interview

1. Turn up late for the interview. Reach at least fifteen minutes before the interview starts.
2. Keep your cell phone switched on. It is very disturbing to

receive phone calls or text messages during an interview.

3. Dress casually, like showing up in casual wear with slippers.

4. Do no homework on an organization before going there. When the interviewer asks, 'What do you know about us,' you should never be in a position where you have to say, 'I don't know much.'

5. Answer, 'I'll let you know after I get the offer,' when asked, 'When can you join?' Always indicate the actual time you would need, for instance, 'within a week', 'within a month,' etc.

6. Set a time limit because of your next appointment. Do not get up from the interview saying, 'Sorry, I have to rush to another meeting. I had budgeted only forty-five minutes for this interview.'

7. Be excessively self-conscious. This is not good, so do not keep adjusting your hair, or keep fidgeting (e.g., moving about in the chair, folding and unfolding your handkerchief, twirling your pen, etc.). This distracts the interviewer. On the other hand, do not get carried away and get over-passionate about any question and talk too much.

8. Talk negatively about any organization, or your family issues. Even if your earlier employer was not fair to you, do not highlight it.

9. Argue with the interviewer.

10. Get emotional during the interview.

15

TECHNICAL INTERVIEWS

Why do companies conduct technical interviews?

After the written technical/domain test, a few candidates are shortlisted for the technical interview. So why do companies assess the technical/domain knowledge twice? The answer is simple. The written test is to test your fundamentals, whether you know the facts/formulae, etc. The technical interview, often conducted by a senior manager, is to assess 'how you think'? Some people are very good in their subject because they are very studious. But if you ask them questions outside the syllabus, they draw a blank. In a job, you cannot predict the technical problems that will arise. So it is important to hire someone who can think on his/her feet and go beyond what he/she knows. Therefore, the technical interviewer will ask you questions like, 'Why do you think this is the correct answer?' If you are able to explain and derive the conclusion based on sound principles and logic, then you will be successful.

The main purpose of a technical interview is to assess your technical aptitude/capability. The main aim of an employer is to assess the following.

How well you know what you know?

It is very important to get your fundamentals right. Being strong in your fundamentals and basics is extremely important.

Interviewers are on the lookout for candidates who have done their homework well. If you are strong in your basics, you will be able to answer any question put up in the interview.

Are you inclined towards learning and performing well?

Employers are totally fine with the fact that you are not aware of the company's work processes, because most of the time what we study is not related to or applicable in the work that we are required to do. But they try to assess if you have the willingness and ability to learn and absorb what is being taught during training sessions.

Do you keep yourself updated on current happenings?

Interviewers like to know if you keep yourself updated with developments that are taking place in various sectors. It is always important that you enhance your general knowledge by reading magazines and newspapers.

How honest are you?

The most common mistake we make is to say that we know something when we don't. Interviewers are people with experience and will easily be able to make out that you are bluffing. In such situations, they drill you until you accept that you do not know the answer. Therefore, instead of beating around the bush, it is always good to accept that you don't know the answer, so that the interviewer can move on to the next question.

How effectively can you communicate and articulate your thoughts?

You may often be asked a variety of questions that are situation-, puzzle- or subject-based. Interviewers assess the clarity with which you answer and articulate your thoughts.

Tips on technical interview preparation and participation

There are various ways you can ace your technical interview. If you are looking for a job in the science, engineering or IT sectors, then you must be ready to face a technical interview. The following are steps that you must take before attending a technical interview.

Undertake research on Google

You must undertake considerable research on the organization, its competitors, technology, work processes, etc. Spend time on the company's website. Interviewers like to test how serious you are about getting the job by asking you questions about the company.

Go back to your basics

Being strong in your fundamentals and basics will always take you a long way. Therefore, revise your basics before you attend a technical interview as it will help you answer questions more confidently.

Solve puzzles/logic problems

Apart from testing your technical aptitude, interviewers also test your analytical skills and creative thinking skills by giving you puzzles to solve, or ask you some logical questions. Therefore, you must practise solving a lot of such questions.

Attend mock interviews

You can ask your friends/family members to act as the interview panel and conduct a mock interview. It will help you assess where you stand and which areas you need to improve.

Talk about your internship projects

You might have done various projects in college. You can refer to one of them in the technical interview and, if given a chance, explain how you selected the topic, how you researched it, how you collected the data, and how you reached a conclusion.

Visit websites that give you information on technical interviews

There are various websites available on the web that can give you information on technical interviews and questions that can be asked. You can also watch mock technical interviews available on YouTube as this will help you prepare well. Some of the websites that can be referred while preparing for a technical interview are listed below.

www.indiabix.com/technical/interview-questions-and-answers
http://jobsearchtech.about.com/od/techinterviews/Technical_
Interview_Questions_and_Tips.htm
www.youtube.com/watch?v=tdTqyalsLt8
www.careercup.com
www.placement.freshersworld.com
http://careerride.com/technical-support-interview-questions.
aspx
www.citehr.com
www.crackaninterview.com

Questions generally asked in technical interviews

It is very difficult to determine what questions can be asked in a technical interview as the technical capability required for every job is different. Nevertheless, in any technical interview, questions will revolve around three words—What, Why and How. We have also conducted research and have shortlisted some general questions that you could come across in a technical interview.

1. What technical certifications do you have?
2. What were/are your strongest subjects in college?
3. How do you think your education will help you in this job?
4. What areas do you think you need to improve in?
5. How good are you with using IT tools?
6. Which programming language are you good at?
7. If given a situation such as (and the interviewer outlines a situation), how will you solve this problem?
8. Are you a creative thinker? If so, can you give us a practical situation where you used your creative thinking abilities?
9. What do you think should be done to improve our work processes?
10. Do you read articles on technology to upgrade your knowledge about latest innovations/happenings? Tell us about the recent books/articles you have read.
11. Tell us about some key projects that you have worked on.

These are very generic questions. You will be asked project- and subject-related questions which are totally subject specific. This is just to give you an idea of what sort of questions can be asked.

For more detailed information, refer to the websites listed above. Please visit these websites to get comprehensive information about questions asked during technical interviews.

Also refer to the last section of the previous chapter on 'Questions you should ask at the end of the interview'.

16

OFFER LETTERS

What is an offer letter?

As a student/fresher, you will attend various campus interviews or interviews after leaving the campus. When this happens, if you clear the assessment and interview stage, you will be given a letter by the company stating that you are selected for so and so position in the company, This is called an offer letter from the company.

Why is an offer letter required?

There is no legal sanctity to an oral offer or even an email offer. Only an offer letter on the company letterhead, signed by an authorized executive, is a valid document.

The offer letter basically contains terms of employment. Once you and the employer sign on the letter, the document is valid and legal.

Always keep in mind that the offer letter becomes a legal document only after you formally accept the offer.

If the employment terms like salary, designation, posting location, etc. are not clear and you want to discuss them, you can do so on the basis of the offer letter. However, if you only have a verbal offer or a two-line email, misunderstandings can arise and harm your further prospects within the company.

An offer letter ensures that if you are travelling from another city, the vacancy will not be filled until you reach.

How is an offer letter different from an appointment letter?

An offer letter is given to you once you are selected after the interview. It explains your position/designation, date of joining, compensation, etc.

An appointment letter is given once you join the company. It confirms that you are on the company's rolls. If you are on probation, then an appointment letter is given at the end of the probation period to confirm your employment. The appointment letter will be based on the offer letter made earlier. The offer letter will automatically expire once the appointment letter is given and accepted by a new employee like you.

Note: Always keep in mind that an offer letter does not give you employee status in the company. It is only after you complete the joining formalities with the organization that you become an official employee.

Here's a sample offer letter.

To
Mr T. Muralidharan   Date: 23 March 2014
Hyderabad

Dear Mr Muralidharan,
This is further to the various meetings and discussions we had last week. We are delighted to offer you the position of recruiter in our organization as per the following terms:
Designation: You will be designated as 'Recruiter'.
Location of Posting: You will be posted at our Corporate Office in Secunderabad.

Position reports to: Head, Executive Search.

Salary and Benefits: Your salary will be in the salary grade of 'Executive' and will include the following:

◌ Total cost to company (CTC) salary of ₹3 lakh per annum;

◌ The above will include basic, HRA, all allowance and retirement benefits. Break-up of the CTC salary will be provided in the appointment letter that will be issued to you after you join; and

◌ Benefits: You will be entitled to mobile phone reimbursement and conveyance reimbursement, as per company policy applicable at your grade. You will also be covered under the Group Accident Insurance Policy of the company and health-care benefits applicable to your grade.

Duties and Responsibilities: The job role requires you to source and recruit ten professionals per month. Detailed list of duties and responsibilities and KRAs will be shared with you along with your appointment letter.

Vacation and Working Days: The company has a five-day week, except the first Saturday of every month which will be a working day. You will be entitled to fourteen days privilege leave and sick leave per year.

Travelling Requirement: Your job does not involve travel except in rare circumstances.

Date of Joining: On or before 1 June 2014. Please communicate your exact date of joining thirty days in advance.

Offer Acceptance: Please sign (in the space specified) and return a duplicate copy of this letter by courier on or before 1 May 2014 to confirm your acceptance of our offer. In case you do not accept this offer as per above, the offer will stand withdrawn automatically on 1 May 2014.

We thank you for your interest in joining our organization. In case you need any assistance/clarification, please contact me at aparna@tminetwork.com

Your Sincerely
Ms Aparna Reddy
Head, HR
Address for correspondence:
B1, Vikrampuri, Secunderabad, 500003
Email ID: hr@tminetwork.com

I accept the offer

_____   _____   _____

(Your Name)   Your Signature   Date

What do you do when you receive an offer letter?

When you receive a job offer, don't just blindly sign it. Take time to read it very carefully. Things that you may have discussed during the interview need not necessarily be there in the offer letter. Therefore, an offer letter must be thoroughly evaluated. Some of the most important things that you must cross-check before accepting the offer are the following.

Job profile

Before accepting the offer, you need to have a clear understanding about what exactly is the job profile, or else, you might end up in the wrong job. So when you are given an option to ask questions in the final interview, the first thing you must ask is, 'What will be my job profile?' If you are not clear and still have doubts about the work, you can always seek clarifications from the concerned person or send them an email stating that you need further clarity regarding the job.

Location of work

Be sure about the location of work. Check out how comfortably you will be able to manage in case you are posted to another city. Check if the company will help you find a place to stay, and allow for transportation time to and from work, etc. in the new location. Also check if the compensation that has been offered is adequate to cover your expenses.

Date of joining

It is important to note when you are expected to join the company, as you may need to make some prior preparations. Therefore, keep in mind all your commitments before accepting the date of joining mentioned in the offer.

Compensation

Yes, it is important that you verify the compensation offered. See if it is in alignment with the discussions that you had during the interview or earlier with the company. Check the variable pay, bonus and your take home pay.

Work timings

This is very crucial as some companies expect you to work in shifts. You should be aware of this.

Travelling clause

Check if your job involves travel. If yes, sit back and think whether you are comfortable with travelling to various locations.

Do your research regarding the company's work culture

You may notice that sometimes, in spite of the salary being good and the timings being comfortable, people are still not comfortable working in an organization. The reason is the work culture. It is extremely important to know how a company treats freshers and what the work culture of the organization is. Therefore, do your research. Talk to people who work for that company and extract all the required information amicably from them.

Discuss with your family

Share the offer letter with your family and seek their support.

Seek clarifications

In case you have any doubt or if you feel you want a change of location of posting, please write a polite letter seeking the change. But do not insist on this change request unless you are willing to forgo the offer. Also, do not expect any revision of salary as a fresher, because companies standardize the pay of freshers and they cannot make an exception only for you.

Communicate your decision

After reviewing all the information, make up your mind—to accept or reject the offer. Either way, communicate the decision formally by email/letter to the employer. It is considered 'unprofessional' to sit on the offer and not communicate. As explained earlier, the employer's offer is binding only if you formally accept the offer.

Rejecting an offer letter

In today's job market, it is difficult to get a job interview, let alone a job, because there are over twenty-five aspirants for every single job and over a hundred aspirants for every single attractive IT job. So think many times before you reject a firm job offer. During the assessment process, you had an opportunity to research the employer and ask questions about the job and salary. Therefore, if the offer is as per discussion, then why should you reject the job?

When should you reject an offer as a fresher?

You can reject an offer in the following circumstances.

- You have multiple offers and you can choose only one, and therefore, reject the remaining offers.
- The company's offer is very different from what was discussed at the interview, and the company is unable to provide satisfactory explanations or the company provided false information during the interview.
- You have received very strong negative information about the company after the interview.
- Do not reject the offer based on the opinion of your friends or on account of salary alone. As mentioned earlier, as a fresher, your skills are very basic, and hence, the company will have to train you and then make you productive. Many companies offer only a stipend during training, which is alright as long as the training provided is very useful.

What do you after you decide to reject an offer?

If you have decided to decline a job offer, then let the employer know in writing that you are declining the offer for so and so reason. Ensure that the letter/mail is polite and to the point. Let the employer know the reason why you are declining the offer. Sometimes, the employer may revise the offer if you make a proper request. Therefore, your rejection may lead to a positive outcome and you may even join the company.

Here's a sample rejection letter/mail:

Ms Aparna Reddy   Date: 5 April 2014
Head, HR

Subject: Inability to accept your offer
Ref.: Your offer dated 13 March 2014 for the position of 'Recruiter'

Dear Madam,

Thank you very much for offering me the Recruiter position. After careful consideration, I regret to inform you that I am declining the offer. You were very encouraging in outlining my future advancement possibilities within the Company but the compensation offered is lower than my need to save enough money to pay back my financial loan. So, I have accepted another opportunity that is more in line with my immediate need. I enjoyed meeting you and the rest of your team. You have been most kind and gracious throughout the interview process and I only wish that circumstances had allowed me to accept your offer. I am confident that we will meet again in the future, and if a suitable opportunity arises, I would love to work with you.

Best wishes for your continued success.

Sincerely,
T. Muralidharan

What to do when you don't receive an offer?

Offer letters are given to candidates who are selected at the interview stage. Sometimes, it may happen that in spite of faring well in the interview, you may not receive an offer. This could be because the employer may not have found what they wanted in your résumé, or maybe they found a better candidate or they want to keep your candidature on hold. So, when you don't receive an offer, don't get dejected or disappointed.

Offers normally take time. Recognize that an offer letter from a company is a serious legal document, and that it takes time for an employer to reach a final decision. Some employers decide immediately after the campus interview. Some employers decide only after all the candidates (across all campuses) are assessed, in which case it may take up to thirty days. In some companies like public sector companies, the offer decision is made by the CEO or by a senior management team who may not be part of the interview, and, this may take even up to forty-five days.

It is a good idea to ask the interview team, after your interview, about when the decision will be communicated, so you can expect the decision within fifteen days of the time committed by them.

Employers usually make three lists—the offer list, the reject list, and the waiting list. The offer list is communicated very quickly because the employer would like to 'block' the candidate and prevent him/her from attending other interviews. The waiting list consists of those who can be upgraded to an offer—if anyone from the offer list declines.

The reject list is normally communicated very late (sometimes it can take ninety days). So if you are on the offer list, you will know quickly. If you do not receive any communication, even after fifteen days of the committed time, then you know that you are on the 'wait list' or 'reject list'.

You can move up to the offer list by following up

If you are on the 'wait list', then you can still get an offer, but if you are on the 'reject list', you cannot expect any offer. So the first thing is to find out whether you are on the 'wait list'. You can do this by writing to the interviewer (if you know his/her name and email ID) or the HR person nominated for processing the result. This is information you must seek at the end of the interview. This is clearly mentioned in the last section of chapter 14 in this book.

Write a polite letter seeking clarification/information on the status of your offer. See the sample below.

Sample follow-up letter

Dear Sir,

Sub: Requesting for communication on my interview outcome

At the outset, I thank you and your organization for giving an opportunity for employment in your organization for the position of 'Recruiter'. This interview and the assessment was completed in a fair manner, but the outcome is yet to be communicated to me. I am very keen on joining your organization and, in fact, I have been researching and updating myself about your organization.

Can I request you to communicate the outcome as early as possible?

Details of my application are given below.

Full Name: T. Muralidharan
Email ID: murali@gmail.com
Position for which I was interviewed: Recruiter
College and city where I was interviewed: Vivekananda College, Chennai
Date of the interview: 15 February 2014
Name of the interviewer: Mr G.K. Kannan (GM & HR)

If there are deficiencies in my application, please let me know. In case my assessment is incomplete and you feel that I should be interviewed again to complete the assessments, I would be very willing. Please let me know.

I look forward to an early communication from you.

Yours sincerely,
T. Muralidharan

Reminder letter

Lastly, it is alright to send a reminder letter with the same content if you do not receive a response. However, after the reminder, if you do not get any response, you should assume that the company is not interested and move on.

Take rejection in your stride

In case you receive a rejection letter or you don't receive any communication even after repeated follow-up, do not take it personally. Typically, only one in eight freshers get an offer after interviews. In case you get it earlier, you are either very good or lucky. Seven do not get it. It is not because the seven are not good. It is because the vacancy is only for one. So forget about this interview, move on and focus on the next interview. But learn from each rejection.

How to learn from rejection letters?

As explained earlier, unless you are very good or lucky, you should expect up to seven rejection letters before you get one good offer. So don't worry, you will get an offer soon, provided you learn and improve with every interview.

Analyze your interview/aptitude test performance

After every aptitude test/interview, write down the mistakes you made, the questions for which you did know the answers. Prepare, so that you do not repeat those mistakes again.

Practise the aptitude tests

If you fail in the aptitude tests, no problem. Practise, join a coaching centre, prepare better, and write the test again after six to nine months.

Review the job roles that you apply for

Many engineers apply for only software jobs despite repeated failures. It does not occur to them that there are many job roles to choose from. For example, in the IT industry, there are many jobs—developer, tester, network engineer, etc. Developer jobs are very much in demand. One in a hundred may get a software developer job in a leading IT company (as against one in eight for a normal job). So apply for that job role where your chances are better.

Review the employer that you apply for

Top employers like Infosys, TCS or big consulting companies are very choosy about the people they select. But for every Infosys, there are over a hundred smaller IT companies willing to hire you. You should join any one of them first, acquire experience and knowledge, and then apply to Infosys again after three to five years. Your chances will be far better then.

Never lose hope

If you are realistic, learn from your mistakes, practice for exams, apply to the correct job and employer, and you will get a job, without fail. Do not lose hope.

17

FIRST NINETY DAYS ON THE RIGHT FIRST JOB

Why are the first ninety days important?

There are three reasons why the first ninety days are the most important days of your work career.

Reason 1: You have to learn on your own

When you were a child, your parents, especially your mother, helped you understand the world around you. She was there to guide you in everything that you did. But there are a few children who are deprived of this wonderful gift by God. So how do they manage? They learn each and every thing on their own. They learn how to live and tackle this competitive world.

The first ninety days on the right first job (RFJ) is like a child without a mother's support. When you are fresh out of college, your mindset is also that of a student. Freshers expect seniors and bosses to guide them through every step of the job. But the reality is different. Once you enter the corporate world, you are all by yourself. You will be provided with some initial training, but that will be only for a limited period. After that, you need to learn the tricks of the trade to survive. So the first ninety days in the RFJ is a very difficult period for any fresher and, if it is not managed well, it can lead to failure in the first job and even impact your career.

Reason 2: You have to move from student life to corporate life

Your transition from a student ethic to an employee ethic is very important. The way you listen, the way you learn, the way you behave in a team, the way you follow the instructions of your boss, the way you dress, the way you speak, etc. are all part of the employee ethic.

When you are a student, you are very informal with other students. Many teaching faculty members are also informal. But when you work in an organization, you will realize that everything is very formal. For example, if you tell your boss that you will submit the report he/she asked for on next Monday at 10 a.m., he/she will take you seriously and expect you to deliver a high quality report at the committed date and time. If you do not deliver the high quality report on time, there will be consequences. But when you are a student working in project teams, your team members will understand if you are not ready with the report on time, or if the quality of the report is not up to the mark. This is just one example of the critical difference between the student work ethic and the employee work ethic. In the first ninety days, you have to successfully complete the transformation from student life to corporate life.

Reason 3: First impressions are very important

First impressions are the best or worst impressions. What does this mean? Your boss and your colleagues decide what kind of person you are, based on what you do in the first ninety days. If you keep your deadlines, if you meet your targets, if you learn to work in teams, than you will be the favourite of your boss and team. If you don't do the above, then your boss and colleagues will start believing that you are not serious about the job or you are not competent. Both these impressions will stay for a long time.

It is important that you leave the best impression on their minds because, as the saying goes, 'The first impression is the last impression.'

The 'honeymoon period' myth

There is always a 'honeymoon period' in the first job—this is actually a very common myth that freshers believe in. Freshers believe that the employer will be lenient to them in the first ninety days because the employer is aware that they are fresh out of college and need time to adjust to the corporate atmosphere. Based on this happy belief of a 'honeymoon period', freshers tend to take the initial days lightly. They think that no one is watching them and their work, but this is a BIG mistake.

You are watched every minute. You must strive hard and put your best foot forward because there is nothing called a 'honeymoon period'. Companies pay you a salary and so they expect output from you. Therefore, you must ensure that you give your best and contribute towards the success of the organization from day one.

How to get the best out of induction training?

When you join your first job, you have a very vague idea of your job role, your company and its products. So you will normally undergo what is called 'induction' training. 'Induction' means 'preparing' you for the job. This training has four parts: (i) company induction; (ii) product induction; (iii) HR induction; and (iv) role induction.

Company induction

It teaches you about the vision and mission of the company, its history, the leadership team, organizational hierarchy, future plans, etc.

Product induction

This is about training you on the products, customer segments, etc. and this training is very elaborate for sales/marketing people.

HR induction

This teaches you about the HR policies of the company, and you will be asked to fill up all the forms for medical insurance, salary bank accounts, provident fund (PF), etc., and you will be told about your entitlements.

Role induction

This is the fourth and the most important. Here, you will be trained on 'how' to do the job, what are the various practices and processes to be followed to succeed in the role, what are the results/targets you are expected to achieve, how to achieve them, how to submit periodic reports to your boss, etc.

Why is training important?

Without proper training, you have to learn on the job. Many of your colleagues may see you as a competitor or may be too busy to teach you. Your boss will also be busy. So you will end up doing your tasks any way that you can, and this will not be the 'best' way of doing them. In training, you will be taught the 'best' way, and this can help you with your tasks from day one.

Things you should do during training

First, 'be attentive' and take the training sessions seriously. Second, participate fully in every activity. Third, 'ask' when you don't understand. This is very important. Do not be shy or worry about what others think. Lastly, be disciplined. Arrive early to classes and stay back if required. Do not be argumentative, but learn to share your different viewpoint in a friendly way. Submit all your reports on time.

About 'on the job' training (OJT)

As discussed earlier, classroom training teaches you how to do things. It gives you the basic knowledge. But OJT gives you practical knowledge about your work and what you can do to excel. In OJT, you learn by doing tasks related to your job. The first letter/email you write, the first report you prepare, the first sale you make, the first presentation you give are all very precious because they teach you the reality.

Take a medical representative's job. When a medical representative takes up his job, he is often accompanied by a senior who introduces him to all the doctors and chemists. Juniors watch their seniors as to how they market/sell their products and learn on the job.

How to get the maximum out of OJT?

First: Respect the person who is training you (called mentor). He/she has the knowledge, experience and, more importantly, also has many other tasks to do. So he/she has to take out time to train you and you must therefore respect the mentor's time.

Second: Ask questions politely. Don't be shy. If you are not able to articulate your question properly, ask for help from the mentor.

Third: Practise the tasks repeatedly. Only by repetition can you become perfect.

Fourth: Try and understand the theory behind the tasks that you do. If your mentor is unable to explain, Google it or ask other co-workers. Only when you know the theory and the practice can you excel.

Finally: Learn from every task that you do.

Typically, how long does the OJT last?

Your OJT can stretch from 15 days to 90 days for most jobs. For some highly technical jobs, it may be for 180 days. The trend is to keep the OJT period as short as possible.

Will there be any targets during OJT?

Yes. But these targets will be lower than targets that will be set for you after the job confirmation.

What pay can I expect during OJT?

During OJT, you can expect a stipend which will be equal or most likely lower than the salary offered. The stipend is mainly to cover your cost of travel and incidental expenses, like lunch, tea, etc. It may not cover your cost of living.

As mentioned earlier in this book, you must be grateful to the employer for giving you the training and OJT, and the benefit of this training and OJT will be far more than the salary reduction.

What happens after the OJT period?

Typically, the company assesses you at the end of the OJT period and decides to do one of the following three things: (i) confirm you in the job; (ii) extend your probation; or (iii) ask you to resign from the job. So the consequence of not taking the OJT seriously may mean that you may lose the job. Extension of your OJT is not good for your career, but it is better than losing the job.

Why is your first boss important?

The boss is the most important person in any job. Let's first understand why the boss is the most important person in your work life. The boss decides your daily work priorities. He/she reviews your work, sets your targets, decides on your incentives, decides your job confirmation, and decides on your promotion. In fact, your boss can decide your future in the company and, even more importantly, your happiness or unhappiness on a daily basis.

You should understand that the boss plays the most important role in your performance management process. Though many aspects of your performance are measurable, there are many aspects which are left to the subjective evaluation of your boss. For example, how well you met your targets may be measurable in a sales job, but in support jobs like HR, finance etc., this is left to the judgement of the boss.

Many people quit their jobs because they don't gel well with their bosses. According to experts, more people quit their jobs because of their boss than any other reason. Unfortunately, they forget that wherever they go, they will always have a boss.

The boss is even more important in your RFJ

Now that you have understood that the 'boss' is important in any job, the role of the boss is much more important in the RFJ. Why?

As explained earlier, the RFJ and its success determines your success in your career, and the first boss determines your success in your RFJ. If he/she is on your side, you will get the best training, the best assignments. The boss can connect you with the right people and give you the right tips on how to survive and succeed.

So, better get the boss on your side.

Guidelines for managing the boss

How to get the boss on your side? Simple. First, understand the boss in totality. What does he want, what makes him happy or unhappy, how does he work, etc.

The following are some tips for managing your boss.

1. Accept that your boss is also human. He/she has likes and dislikes. He/she is emotional and not always rational. Learn to read his/her moods. So you should build two relationships with your boss—professional and personal. The professional relationship means delivering on the job. The personal relationship means he/she likes you, and/or he/she trusts you.

2. Realize your boss also has a boss. So sometimes, he/she is angry with you, not because of what you did but because of what his/her boss did. You need to find out what his/her boss wants and try to deliver to that expectation so that your boss' job becomes easy.

3. Realize that when you meet your targets, the boss also meets his/her targets. So meeting targets—whether it is in sales or in production jobs, or even finance jobs—is the mantra to make your boss happy.

4. Always give credit to your boss. He/she will pay you back through incentives and promotions. Never compete with him/her. When the boss wins in the eyes of his/her boss, he/she will share the victory with you.

5. Never take the boss for granted. He/she may be friendly but he/she expects you to meet the agreed deadlines. In case you cannot meet them, seek permission and renegotiate the deadlines. Don't expect your boss to remind you or followup with you.

6. When the boss asks you to do something, don't increase his/her blood pressure by saying, 'I can't do this.' Always understand what deliverables your boss wants and when. Go back to your seat and figure out how you can deliver as per expectations. If you are overworked, ask him to reschedule other pending jobs. If you need some other person's help, ask the boss to talk to that person. The point is, try to find a way of meeting your boss' expectations before saying 'No'.

7. Learn how to say 'No'. Bosses see 'No' as a sign of insubordination. Ask for more resources (budget, assistants, etc.) and he may say 'No' to these requests, instead of you saying 'No', and that is far better.

8. Don't go to your boss with your problems. He/she is already overwhelmed with his/her own problems. So, go with tentative solutions. Go with a plan.

9. Don't take your co-worker fights to your boss. Bosses believe (many times wrongly) that their team is happy and well-adjusted with each other. So when you go with a complaint, he/she will think you are the cause of team issues. Sort out your colleague issues among yourselves.

10. Ask for feedback. Bosses like that. But take the feedback seriously and show your boss how you have changed as per the feedback.

11. Maintain the confidentiality and trust of the boss. If he confides in you, do not tell others to show off how close the boss is to you. Be very discreet and do not flaunt your boss's friendship.

12. Be a resource person to the boss. Whenever he/she has a special project, he/she should call you. This means he/she thinks you have special skills. Develop expertise in computer skills, like presentations, email, software, etc., because many of the older bosses are weak in computer skills. Similarly, develop expertise in personal finance and personal income tax, and bosses will ask your advice on these matters.

Guidelines for becoming a great team player

When you join any employer and do any job, you will quickly realize that all work is done in teams and by teams. So to succeed in the first job, you need to understand how to work in teams. Your success in your first job also depends upon how you are accepted by your team. Many times, the boss asks team members about their assessment of your work and attitude, and if they say good things about you, it will help you a lot.

Here are some tips.

1. Recognize that the team consists of different types of people with different views. So working in teams requires you to be flexible and to listen to other viewpoints and accept these viewpoints on merit. Respect the other team members.
2. Recognize that every team has a leader, and his job is to drive the team in the right direction. So respect the team leader and try and follow his directions.
3. Communication—clear, frank and open—is essential to earn the trust of team members.
4. Take the initiative and volunteer. If you are the youngest member of the team, you will be expected to volunteer for many tasks.
5. Do not crave credit for your work. Share it with the team.

Your team members will support you right back.

6. Don't get too emotional if you are criticized. Take it positively. Understand the key points and adopt them. Automatically, the team will respect you.

7. Share information and resources freely with other team members. Hoarding information is detrimental to you and the team can gang up against you.

8. Stay positive at all times, especially when your team is struggling to work together. All teams take some time to settle down and do not get worried if your team members are fighting with each other.

18

WHAT TO DO IF YOU ARE IN THE WRONG JOB

When do you start looking for the right first job?

You start the search for your right first job (RFJ) when you discover that you are in the wrong job.

How do you know that you are in the wrong job?

◻ The simplest and easiest way to find out if you are in the wrong job is that you don't feel like going to work when you wake up in the morning.

◻ The next sign that you are in the wrong job is that there is negativity around you. In other words no one in the office talks positively about the future of employees as well as the company.

◻ The third sign is the salary is too low and you are forced to borrow money from your parents, despite living a simple life.

There may be many reasons for all of the above. It may be because the boss is very demanding and difficult. Travelling to and fro to work may be very challenging. You are struggling to cope with the targets, etc. Remember that leaving your first job and first employer is a very serious matter because your entire career will depend on how you succeed in your RFJ. So let's start by analyzing why you want to leave this job.

According to experts, there are three major factors responsible for your disliking the job—(i) company factors; (ii) job factors; and (iii) your own factors. Company factors include boss, colleagues, work culture, compensation, etc. Job-related factors include role mismatch with your personality, too much travel time to and from work, excessive outstation travelling, etc.; while self-related factors include your competency, your attitude, your effort etc.

The first step is to decide which factor among the above three is responsible. If the company is the problem or you are the problem, don't quit the job; stay and improve. If the job role is the problem, analyze why? Is it because your job and personality fitment (please refer to the earlier chapters for JP Fit Test)? If the answer is yes, then you should look for a change of job role within the current employer first, before looking outside.

Please note that the company will do anything—including changing your job location, boss or even job role—only if you succeed in your current job. So to succeed in the current job is the best way to get an internal transfer to another role. Only if this is not possible is it advisable to look for a job change.

How do I make up for the lost time?

First, realize that your career will be for thirty to thirty-five years, from the age of 20–25 till 60. Hence, if you lose one or two years in the wrong job, it does not matter. You can easily make up using the following six steps.

1. Figure out what went wrong so that you can recover lost time.

2. Analyze your behaviour and identify the corrective action that you will take.
3. Identify the right job that fits your personality (we have discussed this in the earlier chapters—please refer to the JP Fit Test).
4. Identify the right employer who can offer you the right job.
5. Research this employer and get the job.
6. Start performing on this new job and thereby recover lost time.

The only way to recover the lost time is to succeed in the right first job (RFJ). You need to do the following to succeed.

Hard work: Double your effort on the job. Work weekends if required.

Smart work: Be up to date on computer skills. Find out how you can use your smart phone better to save time.

Become the boss's favourite: Bosses like people who are both smart and hardworking.

Become an ideal team member: Contribute to the team by doing your part and staying positive.

Enrol: In courses and acquire additional relevant qualifications.

Mohammed Ali (original name, Cassius Clay) is the only three-time World Heavyweight Champion—he won in 1964, 1974 and 1978. In 1967, three years after he won the first title, when he was at the peak of his career, he was jailed because he refused to enrol in the US Army during the Vietnam War. He could not compete for four long years and lost valuable time. But he bounced back due to sheer determination and won back the

World Heavyweight Title—not once but twice, in 1974 and 1978. So this should inspire anyone who loses two to three years on the wrong job.

ACKNOWLEDGEMENTS

There are many people I need to thank. Firstly, Esha Mehan, who started the research on this book. Second, my editor—the one and only Dibakar Ghosh. Lastly, the multitude of job seekers who have shared their pain and anguish of job search with me.

www.ingramcontent.com/pod-product-compliance
Lightning Source LLC
Chambersburg PA
CBHW050123210326
41519CB00015BA/4085